月日は百代の過客にして
行きかふ年もまた旅人なり
舟の上に生涯を浮かべ
馬の口とらへて老いを迎ふる者は
日々旅にして旅を栖とす

芭蕉 おくのほそ道 より

The Narrow Road to Oku

Distributed in the United States by Kodansha America, Inc.,
and in the United Kingdom and continental
Europe by Kodansha Europe Ltd.

Published by Kodansha International Ltd.,
17-14 Otowa 1-chome, Bunkyo-ku Tokyo 112-8652,
and Kodansha America, Inc.

First edition, 1996
05 06 07 08 09 10   15 14 13 12 11 10

www.kodansha-intl.com

The Narrow Road to Oku

おくのほそ道

松尾芭蕉
Matsuo Bashō

ドナルド・キーン［訳］
Translated by Donald Keene

宮田雅之［切り絵］
Illustrated by Miyata Masayuki

KODANSHA INTERNATIONAL
Tokyo • New York • London

序

・

ドナルド・キーン

　松尾芭蕉は1644年に伊賀上野で生まれた。家族は武士階級であったが、生活のために農業を営む程度の水準のようであった。それにもかかわらず武士階級であったために、藩主の子息——町の城に住んでいた藤堂家の人々——とのつながりを生んだ。多分、早熟な才能をいつか披露したことがあったために、この交友関係に入ったのであろう。芭蕉より二歳年長の友人であった藤堂良忠（蝉吟）との関係で傑出した歌人であり歌論家の北村季吟より詩作の手ほどきを受けられることになったのだろう。

　芭蕉の最初の俳句は1662年、彼が十八歳の時に作られた。この頃、初めて宗房という俳号を名乗るようになった。当時の多くの詩人や芸術家ひいては哲学者同様、芭蕉も生涯いくつかの雅号を利用したのである。中で最も著名である芭蕉という雅号は、庭の木からつけられた。1681年、江戸のややさびれた界隈に引っ越しした際、庭の風景を良くするために芭蕉の木を植えたのである。芭蕉は実を結ばないバショウ科の多年生植物で、すぐ風で破れる大きな葉を持っているので、詩人の感受性の象徴であり、俳人の庭にふさわしかった。訪れる人たちは、家を芭蕉庵と呼ぶようになり、程なく芭蕉は自分をこの名で呼ぶようになった。

　芭蕉は1672年に江戸に移った。何故江戸を選んだかよく分からない。或いは俳人として多くの競争の相手があろう京都や大坂より新しい町であった江戸で独立する可能性を見出したのかも知れない。しかし、自身の流派を立てるには数年を要した。流派を立てることは自分の俳句の特色を広め伝えるだけではなく、師として弟子から得る経済的援助や他の面での支援のために欠かせなかった。「おくのほそ道」の冒頭で芭蕉は杉山

PREFACE

·

Donald Keene

Matsuo Bashō was born in 1644 in the town of Ueno, Iga Province. His family was of the samurai class, but of so humble a rank that some of the family may have engaged in agriculture in order to make a living. All the same, belonging to the samurai class made it possible for Bashō to associate with the children of the local aristocracy—members of the Tōdō family who lived in the castle. He probably gained his entrée to this circle of acquaintances by a precocious display of talent on some occasion. Bashō's friendship with Tōdō Yoshitada (Sengin), a boy two years older than himself, enabled him to receive training in poetic composition from an outstanding poet and critic, Kitamura Kigin.

Basho's earliest known haiku was composed in 1662, when he was eighteen. It was about this time that he acquired his first artistic name, Sōbō. Like most other writers, artists, and even philosophers of the time, Bashō was known by various names during the course of his life. The one by which he is best known, Bashō, was derived from a tree in his garden: in 1681, when he moved to a bleak area of the city of Edo, he planted a bashō tree in order to improve the appearance of the garden. The bashō, a variety of banana tree that bears no fruit, had a special meaning for poets: its broad green leaves are easily torn by the wind, a ready symbol for the sensitivity of the poet. Visitors began to refer to the place as the Bashō-an (Cottage of the Bashō Tree), and before long Bashō was using the name for himself.

Bashō first went to live in Edo in 1672. It is not clear why he chose this city. Perhaps he felt he had a better chance of establishing himself in a comparatively new city than in Kyoto or Osaka, where there would be far greater competition from other professional poets, but it took Bashō some years to found his own school of haiku poetry. Founding a school was necessary not only to propagate and preserve a poet's characteristic style, but because as a teacher he would depend on his disciples for financial and other

杉風の別荘に移ったと書いたが、杉風は富裕の商人で、芭蕉が金銭的に困った折、何回も援助を与えた。芭蕉は1680年に弟子たちの作品集を出版したが、それまでに、彼の流派が確立していたことを物語っている。

　1684年に芭蕉は生涯における記念碑と呼ぶべき五つの紀行文のきっかけとなった最初の旅に出かけた。前年伊賀上野で死んだ母の墓に参るというのが表向きの理由であったのだが、旅の間の体験が自分の俳句に新たな啓示を与えるだろうとみこしていたに違いない。又、数々の町への訪問は「蕉風」を広め、それまで他の流派に属していた俳人を惹き付けるためでもある。

　五つの紀行文の最後を飾る1689年の旅行を描いた「おくのほそ道」は芭蕉の最高傑作であるのみならず、日本古典文学の代表作の一つでもある。日本の高校生なら少なくとも抜粋を読んだことがあろう。高校生等の初心者に芭蕉の作風の難解さを解説する出版物は山とある。又、ヨーロッパの何ヵ国語かの翻訳ができていて、日本語の俳句や俳文が持つ特質を翻訳の困難を乗り越えて美しく伝えるものもある。

　日本文学のほとんどの作品の翻訳は、日本語に長けた者にさえ困難である。訳者を常に困らせる二つの例をあげよう。それは先ず、単数と複数の区別そして定義と不定の区別の欠如である。これらにより、作者が本当に何を意図していたのか訳者が決断を下すことになる。作者が存命なら教えてもくれるがいつもそうはいかない。私が安部公房の「緑色のストッキング」を訳していた時、ストッキングは単数か複数かを聞いたところ、安部さんはただ笑い、それは訳者の問題で自分とは関係ないと言われたのである。

　「おくのほそ道」のような古典文学の作品の翻訳は現代文学の翻訳より遥かにむずかしい。先ずぶつかるのは、「おくのほそ道」という題名の翻訳である。その言葉は原文に一度現れる。

　「かの画図にまかせてたどり行ば、おくの細道の山際に十符の菅あり。」

support. At the opening of *Oku no Hosomichi*, Bashō mentions moving to the villa belonging to Sugiyama Sampū, the rich merchant who proved again and again a generous patron when Bashō was in financial need. In 1680 Bashō published a collection of poetry composed by his pupils, a sign that his school had been solidly established.

In 1684 Bashō set out on a journey that occasioned the first of five narratives that stand as milestones in his career. The ostensible purpose of this journey was to pay his respects at the grave of his mother, who had died in Ueno in the previous year, but (as he no doubt foresaw) his experiences during his travels would inspire many poems. His visits to different towns would also serve to make his school of haiku better known, and attract haiku poets who had previously been affiliated with another school.

Of the five travel diaries describing his journeys, the last, *Oku no Hosomichi*, written in 1689, is not only the best but is considered one of the major texts of classical Japanese literature. Every Japanese who has attended high school will have read at least excerpts from this work, and there are over a hundred commentated editions to help beginners over the difficulties of Bashō's style. There are also translations into various European languages, some of them quite beautiful despite the difficulty of conveying the special qualities of Japanese poetry and poetic prose.

Almost any Japanese work of literature is difficult to translate, even for someone who has thorough competence in the language. To cite two examples that constantly put the translator on his mettle: the lack of distinction in Japanese between singular and plural, and between definite and indefinite, make it necessary for the translator to decide what the author really meant. If the author is still alive, he may help, but not always. When I was translating *Midori iro no sutokkingu* by Abe Kōbō, I asked him whether this should be The Green Stocking or The Green Stockings, but he only smiled and commented that this was my problem, not his.

The problems of translating a work of classical literature such as *Oku no Hosomichi* are far more complicated. The first problem in this instance is how to translate the title. The words oku no hosomichi occur at one place in the text: "kano ezu ni makasete tadoriyukaba, oku no hosomichi no yamagiwa ni tofu no suge ari." A more-or-less literal translation would be something like, "As

これを直訳するとこうなる。

"As [we] trudged ahead, following the above-mentioned picture-map, there was along the edge of the mountain [bordering] the narrow road to Oku the ten-strand sedge."

英語で読むと何のことかわからない。「十符の菅」は特に困惑を招く。十本という数では生えず（あるいは何本でも）それが山のそばにあるというのも不十分である。そこにあるというのはともかく、実をなしていたのかわからず、大体そのような付けたしがあったところで道から遠く離れた山のそばにすげがあったのか道そのものにあったのか明確にするものではない。そしてborderingという言葉を取れば――原文にはないのだが――三つの要素すなわち、山のそば、細い道、そしてすげの関係はいよいよあいまいとなる。そして原文では果たして誰がとぼとぼ歩いていたのか書かれていない。

「おくのほそ道」を現代の日本語に訳す難しさはほとんど西洋の諸国語にうつしかえるかのようである。「加右衛門の描いてくれた絵図に従って行くと、奥の細道と呼ばれる細い街道があり、その街道の山側に添って、古歌で有名な十符の菅が生えていた。」

こう書くと原文よりはっきりするが、照らし合わせればそれが芭蕉の俳文の美をだいなしにした結果というのがわかる。言うまでもなく、芭蕉は「古歌で有名なる」と書かなかった。又、読者たち（現代の読者と違い）が菅で織られた木目の粗いむしろ（片方に十本の網目）が古くから度々歌われてきたのを知っているだろうと芭蕉は思ったに違いない。

元の問題に戻ろう。題名をどう訳すべきか。以前私はThe Narrow Road of Okuと訳したことがある。間違いではないものの、啓発的だとは言いがたい。疑いなく芭蕉はその名の特定の道にふれていたが、この道は作品にほとんど現れないのである。「奥という地方に入る細道」として訳した方がましかも知れない。つまり芭蕉の目的地は本州の北端にある国

[we] trudged ahead, following the above-mentioned picture-map, there was along the edge of the mountain [bordering] the narrow road to Oku the ten-strand sedge."

Read in English, the sentence does not make much sense. Mention of "ten-strand sedge" is particularly baffling because sedge does not grow in clumps of ten (or any other number). The statement that the sedge was "along the edge of the mountain" is insufficient; one would expect to be informed that the sedge was growing there, or that it was harvested there, but even making such an addition to the text still does not clarify whether the sedge was growing at a distance from the road at the edge of a mountain, or along the road itself. And if the word "bordering" is omitted—it does not occur in the text—the relationships among the three elements—the edge of the mountain, the narrow road, and the sedge—become even vaguer. Finally, the original text does not indicate the subject of the sentence—who was trudging ahead.

The problem of translating *Oku no Hosomichi* into modern Japanese is almost as great as translating it into a European language. Here is a translation into English, again more-or-less literal, from a modern Japanese version: "As [we] walked ahead following the picture-map that Kaemon had drawn for us, there was the narrow road which is called Oku no Hosomichi. Along the mountain-side of the road the 'ten-strand sedge,' famous from old poetry, was growing."

This is certainly clearer than the translation from the original text, but if one looks back at the original, one sees immediately that the clarity has been obtained by destroying the beauty of Bashō's prose. Obviously, he would not have written "famous from old poetry." He would also have assumed that his readers (though not readers of today!) would be familiar with the coarsely woven matting (ten meshes to a side) made of sedge that is often mentioned in old poetry.

But to return to the original question: how is one to translate the title? I have in the past called the work "The Narrow Road of Oku," a safe but not illuminating translation. Bashō was undoubtedly referring to the road of that name, but not only to the road, which hardly figures in the work. "The Narrow Road into Oku" might be better, suggesting that Bashō's destination was Oku, the general

であった。又、それは奥地あるいは奥に引っ込んだ場所という地理的な意味と共にこの旅が俳句の世界の深淵に入っていくという比喩的な意味においてもふさわしいかも知れない。芭蕉が何を意図したのか我々には知るよしもないが、これらすべてだったかも知れない。翻訳にまつわる困難が題名の翻訳だけでもわかる。

しかし、このように難点をあげるのは、誤解を招くかも知れない。そのわかりにくさにもかかわらず、「おくのほそ道」は難解な詩的表現を喜ぶ学生だけではなく、十符の菅やその他の詩的引喩が理解できない一般読者にも愛されている。極端に集中された散文は少なくとも最初は解説なしには読みにくいが、それが醸し出す詩的余韻はみごとなものである。

散文よりもさらに困難な翻訳は作品全体にちりばめられた俳句である。たった十七字という短さゆえひとことひとことが必要であって暗示にことさら重きが置かれる。芭蕉の紀行文中の散文は俳句の意味を明確にすることが度々あるが、曖昧さが残る。「おくのほそ道」の最初の句は特に訳しにくい。

　　　　草の戸も住み替る代ぞひなの家

文字通りに訳せばこうなる。

An age in which the occupant of a grass hut changes—a house of dolls.

この英訳を読んで俳句の意味を理解する人は恐らく一人もいない。原文もなかなか分かりにくいが、一度説明されると、芭蕉の表現の簡潔さに驚く他はない。俳文が教えるように、芭蕉が住み慣れたわらぶきの小屋を離れていくのが示唆される。次の住人は芭蕉とは違い家族を持った男であろう。そして家の性格も新しい住人と共にかわる。三月三日のひな祭りには小さな人形が飾られるであろう。

name for the provinces at the northern end of the island of Honshū. Oku also means "interior" or "inner recesses," and this meaning would also be appropriate, both geographically, indicating that Bashō's travels would take him to the inner recesses of the country, and metaphorically, suggesting that his journey was to an inner world, probably the world of haiku poetry. We shall never know which of these meanings Bashō intended; perhaps he meant all of them. The difficulty of translating the title is typical of the whole.

To point out these difficulties, however, may be misleading. Despite the difficulties, *Oku no Hosomichi* is loved not only by scholars who delight in recondite poetic lore but by quite ordinary readers, even if they have no idea of the meaning of "ten-strand sedge" or any of the other poetic references. The extreme sparseness of the prose makes it difficult to read without a commentary, at least on first encounter, but it also makes the work a miracle of poetic overtones.

Even more difficult to translate than the prose are the haiku scattered throughout the work. Because the haiku is so short— only seventeen syllables—every word counts, and there is the utmost reliance on suggestion. In Bashō's travel diaries the prose often helps to clarify the meaning of the haiku, but even so, there are ambiguities. The first haiku of *Oku no Hosomichi* is particularly difficult to translate.

kusa no to mo
sumikawaru yo zo
hina no ie

A fairly literal translation would be something like: "An age in which the occupant of a grass hut changes—a house of dolls."

No one would be likely to guess the meaning from such an English translation. The original poem is almost as hard to understand, but once the meaning is explained, no matter how prosaically, one can only marvel at Bashō's economy of language. As we know from the prose, he was about to leave the simple dwelling ("grass hut") where he had lived. The next occupant, unlike Bashō, would be a man with a family, and the character of the house itself would change with the new occupants: on the third day of the third month it would be decorated with rows of little dolls in honor of the Girls' Festival.

すべての俳句が難解ではないが、解釈について二つ以上の可能性があるという俳句は実に多い。「おくのほそ道」に収められた俳句には芭蕉の大傑作が何句もある。しかし、ほとんどの句は芭蕉の心にひらめいたものではないのである。「おくのほそ道」は奥から江戸への帰還より五年の歳月をかけて完成させ、とりわけ俳句にはいくつかの変形があった。現今に残る形に達するまで芭蕉は何度も俳句を作り直した。

「更科紀行」には宿におけるおかしな一幕がある。旅の一日を終えた芭蕉はその日の景色を俳句に作ろうとするが、彼が苦しむ様子を見ている「道心の坊」が芭蕉を慰めんとし、「わかき時おがみめぐりたる地、阿弥陀のたふとき数をつくし」その結果、芭蕉の詩的ひらめきは完全に閉ざされた、と芭蕉が物語る。「おくのほそ道」の完成までに、多くの苦しみを経たことは疑いない。

「おくのほそ道」の永年にわたる人気は一つ一つの俳句に負うところが多いが、散文の方も劣らず称賛されている。冒頭や松島と象潟への訪問の描写は特に有名であるが、他にも同じく美しい部分がある。一方では、おだやかにまとめられた部分もある。芭蕉は連歌の伝統を守って、ある句の前後に余り叙情的でない句を置くことによって、宝石の連なりで読者に疲労を与えないように配慮を施した。

何世紀もの間、日本人の旅行の主要な目的の一つは歌枕を見ることであった。和歌に現れる場所の数々が芭蕉を長い旅にかりたてたようである。それゆえ、彼は時に和歌について無学の輩が見落とすような場所を見るためにも、長い回り道をした。そして、芭蕉が訪れた場所の描写あるいは俳句は、数えきれない日本人（そして外国人も）をそれぞれの旅に駆り立てた。

芭蕉は道連れであった曾良にわずかに触れるが、自分の名や職業、そして「道祖神のまねきに会」ったこと以外に、何故長くて時につらい旅に出

Not all the haiku are so difficult to understand, but there is hardly one that has not been given an alternate explanation. At the same time, the haiku included in *Oku no Hosomichi* are among the finest Bashō composed. Most of them, however, did not spring into Bashō's head exactly in the same form in which they appear in the finished work. The text we have of *Oku no Hosomichi* was not completed by Bashō until about five years after his return from Oku, and we know of variants, especially in the haiku. He undoubtedly revised the work many times before it reached its present state.

In one of Bashō's early travel diaries, *Journey to Sarashina*, there is a funny scene at an inn where Bashō, after a day of travel, is trying to beat into shape haiku that have occurred to him that day. An old priest, observing Bashō in apparent anguish, supposes that he has suffered some tragedy, and tries to console him with accounts of the miracles of Amida Buddha. As a result, Bashō tells us, his poetic impulse was completely blocked. No doubt many moans accompanied the creation and re-creation of the haiku in *Oku no Hosomichi*.

The great popularity of *Oku no Hosomichi* owes much to the popularity of the individual haiku, but the prose is no less admired. The opening and the accounts of Bashō's visits to Matsushima and Kisakata are especially well-known sections, but there are others almost as beautiful. Still other sections are low-keyed. Bashō, observing the traditions of renga (linked verse), included sections that are conspicuously less lyrical than those before and after, seemingly in order not to exhaust the reader with an unbroken series of gemlike vignettes.

For centuries one of the chief reasons that Japanese had for travel was to see uta-makura, places that are mentioned in poetry, and this probably was Bashō's ultimate reason for making his long journey. This is why he sometimes took long detours to see places which might seem to someone ignorant of their poetic background to be of no interest. Bashō's descriptions of the places he visited, even those memorable only because of legends or poems connected with them, have in turn inspired innumerable Japanese (and even some non-Japanese) to travel and see them with their own eyes.

Although Bashō briefly describes Sora, his companion during much of the journey, he does not mention his own name nor give

たか、一切の釈明をしていない。だが、結局は遠回しに自らを語るのである。そして、つまるところ、「おくのほそ道」から湧き出るその芭蕉像が作品の人気のやむところのない源泉なのである。

　言うまでもなく、芭蕉は自然の美に非常に敏感であったが、旅の道中出会った人々も温かく描写した。そして、過去は現在にもまして彼と共にあった。俳句や俳文に託したものには、永遠の輝きがひめられている。

　芭蕉が燦然と描いた多くの風景が近年消えつつあるが、それらの美は「おくのほそ道」に今も息づいている。将来も変わることなく人々を彼の詩の深淵にいざない続けることであろう。

any indication of his profession or what reasons—apart from wan-
derlust—inspired him to make a long and sometimes painful jour-
ney. He nevertheless indirectly tells us much about himself, and
ultimately, the self-portrait of Bashō that emerges from *Oku no
Hosomichi* may be the most compelling reason for its popularity.

He was, of course, highly sensitive to the beauty of nature,
but he also described with warmth the people he met on the way,
and the past, no less than the present, was always with him. His
impressions, whether expressed in poetry or prose, have timeless
validity.

Even though many of the landscapes Bashō so magically
described have been defaced in recent years, their beauty lives on
in *Oku no Hosomichi* and will doubtless continue to stir future
generations with the desire to accompany Bashō on his journey to
the inner recesses of poetry.

〈序 章〉

月日は百代の過客にして、行かふ年も又旅人也。舟の上に生涯をうかべ馬の口とらえて老をむかふる物は、日々旅にして、旅を栖とす。古人も多く旅に死せるあり。予もいづれの年よりか、片雲の風にさそはれて、漂泊の思ひやまず、海浜にさすらへ、去年の秋江上の破屋に蜘の古巣をはらひて、や、年も暮、春立る霞の空に、白川の関こえんと、そゞろ神の物につきて心をくるはせ、道祖神のまねきにあひて取もの手につかず、も、引の破をつゞり、笠の緒付かえて、三里に灸すゆるより、松島の月先心にかゝりて、住る方は人に譲り、杉風が別墅に移るに、

草の戸も住替る代ぞひなの家

面八句を庵の柱に懸置。

18

The months and days are the travellers of eternity. The years that come and go are also voyagers. Those who float away their lives on ships or who grow old leading horses are forever journeying, and their homes are wherever their travels take them. Many of the men of old died on the road, and I too for years past have been stirred by the sight of a solitary cloud drifting with the wind to ceaseless thoughts of roaming.

Last year I spent wandering along the seacoast. In autumn I returned to my cottage on the river and swept away the cobwebs. Gradually the year drew to its close. When spring came and there was mist in the air, I thought of crossing the Barrier of Shirakawa into Oku. I seemed to be possessed by the spirits of wanderlust, and they all but deprived me of my senses. The guardian spirits of the road beckoned, and I could not settle down to work.

I patched my torn trousers and changed the cord on my bamboo hat. To strengthen my legs for the journey I had moxa burned on my shins. By then I could think of nothing but the moon at Matsushima. When I sold my cottage and moved to Sampū's villa, to stay until I started on my journey, I hung this poem on a post in my hut:

kusa no to mo	Even a thatched hut
sumikawaru yo zo	May change with a new owner
hina no ie	Into a doll's house.[1]

This became the first of an eight-verse sequence.

草の戸も住替る代ぞひなの家

Even a thatched hut
May change with a new owner
Into a doll's house.

〈旅立〉

　弥生も末の七日、明ぼのゝ、空朧々として、月は在明にて光おさまれる物から、不二の峰幽にみえて、上野・谷中の花の梢、又いつかはと心ぼそし。むつましきかぎりは宵よりつどひて、舟に乗て送る。千じゆと云所にて船をあがれば、前途三千里のおもひ胸にふさがりて、幻のちまたに離別の泪をそゝぐ。

行春や鳥啼魚の目は泪

　是を矢立の初として、行道なをすゝまず。人々は途中に立ならびて、後かげのみゆる迄はと、見送なるべし。

〈草加〉

　ことし元禄二とせにや、奥羽長途の行脚、只かりそめに思ひたちて、呉天に白髪の恨を重ぬといへ共、耳にふれていまだめに見ぬさかひ、若生て帰らばと定なき頼の末をかけ、其日漸草加と云宿にたどり着にけり。痩骨の肩にかゝれる物先くるしむ。只身すがらにと出立侍を、帋子一衣は夜の防ぎ、ゆかた・雨具・墨・筆のたぐひ、あるはさりがたき餞などしたるは、さすがに打捨がたくて、路次の煩となれるこそわりなけれ。

〈室の八島〉

　室の八島に詣す。同行曾良が曰、「此神は木の花さくや姫の神と申て富士一躰也。無戸室に入て焼給ふちかひのみ中に、火々出見のみこと生れ給ひしより室の八島と申。又煙を読習し侍もこの謂也」。将、このし

22

When I set out on the twenty-seventh of the third month*² the dawn sky was misty. The early morning moon had lost its light, but the peak of Fuji could faintly be seen. The cherry blossoms on the boughs at Ueno and Yanaka stirred sad thoughts as I wondered when again I might see them. My dearest friends had all come to Sampū's house the night before so that they might accompany me on the boat part of the way. When we disembarked at a place called Senju, the thought of the long journey ahead filled me with emotion. I stood at the crossway of parting in this dreamlike existence and wept tears of farewell:

yuku haru ya	Spring is passing by!
tori naki uo no	Birds are weeping and the eyes
me wa namida	Of fish fill with tears.

I set out after composing this verse, the first of my journey, but I could barely keep going ahead, for when I looked back I saw my friends standing in a row, no doubt to watch until we were lost to sight.

This year, the second of the Genroku era,*³ the thought somehow crossed my mind that I might take a walking trip all the way to distant Oku. It did not matter if I should be unlucky enough to grow gray on my travels, for I wanted to see places I had long heard about but never visited. It seemed to me instead that I should be fortunate if I managed to come home alive. Leaving this uncertainty for the future to decide, I pursued my journey to a post-town called Sōka which we were barely able to reach the day of our departure.

The first pain I suffered on the journey came from the weight of the pack on my scrawny shoulders. I had intended when I set out to carry nothing at all, but I needed a set of paper clothes to protect me from the cold of night. Then there were such things as a bathrobe, rainwear, pen and ink, and the like, as well as parting gifts that I could not very well refuse or throw away. They were a bother on the journey, but there was nothing I could do about them.

We paid a visit to the Doorless Shrine of the Cauldron. My companion, Sora, told me its story. "The goddess of this shrine is called Princess Flowering Blossoms, the same as at Mount Fuji. The shrine has been known as Doorless ever since she entered it, walled herself in, and then gave birth to Prince Fire Bright among

行春や鳥啼魚の目は泪

Spring is passing by!
Birds are weeping and the eyes
Of fish fill with tears.

ろといふ魚を禁ず。縁起の旨世に伝ふ事も侍し。

〈仏五左衛門〉

　卅日、日光山の麓に泊る。あるじの云けるやう、「我名を仏五左衛門と云。万正直を旨とする故に、人かくは申侍ま、一夜の草の枕も打解て休み給へ」と云。いかなる仏の濁世塵土に示現して、か、る桑門の乞食順礼ごときの人をたすけ給ふにやと、あるじのなす事に心をとゞめてみるに、唯無智無分別にして正直偏固の者也。剛毅木訥の仁に近きたぐひ、気稟の清質、尤尊ぶべし。

〈日 光〉

　卯月朔日、御山に詣拝す。往昔、此御山を「二荒山」と書しを、空海大師開基の時、「日光」と改給ふ。千歳未来をさとり給ふにや、今此御光一天にか、やきて、恩沢八荒にあふれ、四民安堵の栖穏なり。猶、憚多くて筆をさし置ぬ。

　　あらたうと青葉若葉の日の光

　　黒髪山は霞か、りて、雪いまだ白し。

　　剃捨て黒髪山に衣更　　　曾良

the flames she had lit to prove her fidelity. That is why, also, the poets always mention the smoke."[4]

It is forbidden here to eat the fish called konoshiro.[5] The main features of the history of this shrine are widely known.

On the thirtieth of the third month we stopped at the foot of Nikkō Mountain. The innkeeper informed us, "My name is Buddha Gozaemon. People call me Buddha because I am so honest in everything I do, so even if you are staying just one night, please relax and make yourselves at home." Curious as to what kind of Buddha had appeared in this world of foulness and corruption to protect such beggar-pilgrims as ourselves, I observed our host's behavior, and saw that although he was ignorant and clumsy, he was honesty itself, one of those described by Confucius as being "strong, simple, and slow to speak—such a one is near to Goodness." His purity of heart was indeed most admirable.

On the first day of the fourth month we worshipped at the sacred mountain. In ancient times the name of this mountain was written Nikō, but when the Great Teacher Kūkai founded a temple here he changed the name to Nikkō, or Sunlight. I wonder if he was able to look into the future a thousand years later. Now its holy light shines throughout the realm, and its blessings overflow to the remotest corners. The four classes live in peace and security. But here, with due reverence, I must lay down my pen.[6]

ara tōto	How awe-inspiring!
aoba wakaba no	On the green leaves, the young leaves
hi no hikari	The light of the sun.

Kurokami-yama (Black Hair Mountain) was mist-enshrouded, and the snow was still white.

sorisutete	I shaved off my hair,
kurokamiyama ni	And now at Black Hair Mountain
koromogae	It's time to change clothes.[7]

Sora

暫時は滝に籠るや夏の初

For a little while
I'll shut myself inside the falls—
Summer retreat has begun.

曾良は河合氏にして惣五郎と云へり。芭蕉の下葉に軒をならべて、予が薪水の労をたすく。このたび松しま・象潟の眺共にせん事を悦び、且は羈旅の難をいたはらんと、旅立暁髪を剃て墨染にさまをかえ、惣五を改て宗悟とす。仍て黒髪山の句有。「衣更」の二字、力ありてきこゆ。

廿余丁山を登つて滝有。岩洞の頂より飛流して百尺、千岩の碧潭に落たり。岩窟に身をひそめ入て、滝の裏よりみれば、うらみの滝と申伝え侍る也。

暫時は滝に籠るや夏の初

〈那須〉

那須の黒ばねと云所に知人あれば、是より野越にかゝりて、直道をゆかんとす。遥に一村を見かけて行に、雨降日暮。農夫の家に一夜をかりて、明れば又野中を行。そこに野飼の馬あり。草刈おのこになげきよれば、野夫といへども、さすがに情しらぬには非ず。「いかゞすべきや。されども此野は縦横にわかれて、うゐうゐ敷旅人の道ふみたがえん、あやしう侍れば、此馬のとゞまる所にて馬を返し給へ」とかし侍ぬ。ちいさき者ふたり、馬の跡したひてはしる。独は小姫にて、名を「かさね」と云。聞なれぬ名のやさしかりければ、

かさねとは八重撫子の名成べし　　　曾良

頓て人里に至れば、あたひを鞍つぼに結付て馬を返しぬ。

30

Sora's family name is Kawai, and his personal name is Sōgorō. He built his house alongside the lower leaves of my bashō tree,*⁸ and helped me with firewood and water for my kitchen. On this occasion he was delighted at the thought of sharing with me the sights of Matsushima and Kisakata. At the same time, he thought he would be able to spare me the hardships of travel. Early on the morning of our departure he shaved his head and changed to somber robes of black. He also changed the characters used in writing his name to others with Buddhist overtones. That is why he composed the poem about Black Hair Mountain. I thought that the words "change clothes" were particularly effective.

We climbed a mile or so up the mountain to a waterfall that cascaded a hundred feet from the roof of a cave down into an azure pool lined with a thousand stones. By crawling into the cave one gets the view of the waterfall from behind that gives it the name of "Rear View Falls."

shibaraku wa	For a little while
taki ni komoru ya	I'll shut myself inside the falls—
ge no hajime	Summer retreat has begun.*⁹

I have an acquaintance at a place called Kurobane [Black Wing] in Nasu, and thought I would take a short cut there through the fields from Nikkō. It began to rain and grow dark as we walked, our eyes set on a village in the distance. We hired lodgings for the night at a farmer's house. When it grew light, we again set out through the fields. We saw a horse pasturing there, and begged help from a farmer cutting hay. He was only a rough, country fellow, but he was not without feelings. He said, "Let me see—what would be your best plan? These fields here go off in every which way. You're travellers and don't know the place, so you could easily get lost. That worries me. Just send back this horse wherever he stops." With this, he lent us the horse.

Two children ran along behind the horse. One of them was a little girl named Kasane [Double]. The unusual name was so charming that Sora composed this poem:

Kasane to wa	Double—that must be
yaenadeshiko no	The name somebody gave to
na naru beshi	A double-petalled pink.*¹⁰

Before long we reached a village where I sent back the horse with some money tied to its saddle.

31

かさねとは八重撫子（やへなでしこ）の名成（な）るべし

Double—that must be
The name somebody gave to
A double-petalled pink.

〈黒羽〉

黒羽の館代浄坊寺何がしの方に音信る。思ひがけぬあるじの悦び、日夜語つゞけて、其弟桃翠など云が、朝夕勤とぶらひ、自の家にも伴ひて、親属の方にもまねかれ、日をふるまゝに、ひとひ郊外に逍遥して、犬追物の跡を一見し、那須の篠原をわけて、玉藻の前の古墳をとふ。それより八幡宮に詣。与市扇の的を射し時、「別しては我国氏神正八まん」とちかひしも、此神社にて侍と聞ば、感応殊しきりに覚えらる。暮れば桃翠宅に帰る。

修験光明寺と云有。そこにまねかれて、行者堂を拝す。

　　　夏山に足駄を拝む首途哉

We called at the house of one Jōbōji, the deputy governor of the castle at Kurobane. The master was delighted by the unexpected visit, and we had much to talk about, day and night. His younger brother, Tōsui, called on us assiduously at all hours, and invited us to his house. We were also invited to the houses of their relatives, and in this way the days piled up. One day we went for a stroll outside the town to have a look at the remains of the dog-hunting track. We pushed our way through the bamboo grove of Nasu, and paid our respects to the old tomb of Lady Tamamo. From there we went to worship at the Hachiman Shrine. I was particularly moved when I learned that this was the very shrine to which Yoichi had prayed addressing himself "especially to Shō Hachiman, the tutelary deity of my native province" before he shot his arrow at the fan.[11] It grew dark, and we returned to Tōsui's house.

There is a yamabushi [mountain ascetic] temple called Kōmyō-ji nearby. I was invited there and worshipped in the Hall of the Ascetic:

natsuyama ni	In summer mountains
ashida wo ogamu	I bow before his high clogs—
kadode kana	My journey's just begun.[12]

夏山に足駄を拝む首途哉

In summer mountains
I bow before his high clogs—
My journey's just begun.

〈雲巌寺〉

当国雲岸寺のおくに、仏頂和尚山居跡あり。

竪横の五尺にたらぬ草の庵

むすぶもくやし雨なかりせば

と、松の炭して岩に書付侍りと、いつぞや聞え給ふ。其跡みんと雲岸寺に杖を曳ば、人々すゝんで共にいざなひ、若き人おほく道のほど打さはぎて、おぼえず彼麓に到る。山はおくあるけしきにて、谷道遥に、松杉黒く苔したゞりて、卯月の天今猶寒し。十景尽る所、橋をわたって山門に入。

さて、かの跡はいづくのほどにやと、後の山によぢのぼれば、石上の小菴岩窟にむすびかけたり。妙禅師の死関、法雲法師の石室をみるがごとし。

木啄も庵はやぶらず夏木立

と、とりあへぬ一句を柱に残侍し。

38

The remains of the hut in which the priest Butchō[13] lived are in the mountain behind the Ungan Temple in this province.

tate yoko no	It was a nuisance
goshaku ni taranu	Even to tie together
kusa no io	This little grass hut,
musubu mo kuyashi	Not five feet long or wide—
ame nakariseba	If only it never rained!

Butchō once told me that he had written this poem with pinewood charcoal on a rock. I thought I should like to see what remained of his hut and set out, walking-stick in hand, for the Ungan Temple. Some men offered to show the way. Most of them were young, very lively company, and before we knew it we had reached the foot of the mountain.

Mountains stretched out as far as one could see. Along a valley path that led into the distance, moss dripped from the darkly clustering pines and cedars. The sky, though it was summer, was still cold. When we had passed the last of the Ten Famous Views, we crossed a bridge and entered the temple gate. Wondering where the remains of Butchō's dwelling might be, I scrambled up the mountain behind the temple, and there I found, on top of a rock, a small lean-to built onto a cave. It was as if I were looking on the Death Barrier of Myō zenji or the stone chamber of Hōun hōshi.[14]

kitsutsuki mo	Even woodpeckers
io wa yaburazu	Do not harm this little hut
natsu kodachi	Perched in summer trees.

I left this impromptu verse on a post in the hut.

木啄も庵はやぶらず夏木立

Even woodpeckers
Do not harm this little hut
Perched in summer trees.

〈殺生石・遊行柳〉

是より殺生石に行。館代より馬にて送らる。此口付のおのこ、「短冊得させよ」と乞。やさしき事を望侍るものかなと、

野を横に馬牽むけよほとゝぎす

殺生石は温泉の出る山陰にあり。石の毒気いまだほろびず、蜂・蝶のたぐひ、真砂の色の見えぬほどかさなり死す。

又、清水ながるゝの柳は、蘆野の里にありて、田の畔に残る。此所の郡守戸部某の、「此柳みせばや」など、折々にの給ひ聞え給ふを、いづくのほどにやと思ひしを、今日此柳のかげにこそ立より侍つれ。

田一枚植て立去る柳かな

From there we went to the "life-taking stones." I was sent off on a horse, by courtesy of the deputy governor. The man leading the horse asked me to write a poem-card for him. "What an elegant thing for him to want!" I thought, and wrote:

no wo yoko ni	Lead the horse sideways
uma hikimuke yo	Across the meadows—I hear
hototogisu	A nightingale.

The life-taking stones are situated on high ground near where a hot spring gushes. The fumes emanating from the rocks have still not lost their poison. So many dead bees, butterflies and suchlike insects had piled up that one couldn't tell the color of the sand.

The willow tree where "flows a crystal stream"[*15] stands on a path through the rice fields near Ashino Village. The prefect of the district, a certain secretary, had often said he would like to show me the willow, and I wondered where it might be. Today I stood in the shade of the very tree.

ta ichimai	They sowed a whole field,
uete tachisaru	And only then did I leave
yanagi kana	Saigyō's willow tree.

田一枚植て立去る柳かな

They sowed a whole field,
And only then did I leave
Saigyō's willow tree.

〈白川の関〉

　心許なき日かず重るま〻に、白川の関にか〻りて旅心定りぬ。「いかで都へ」と便求しも断也。中にも此関は三関の一にして、風騒の人心をとゞむ。秋風を耳に残し、紅葉を俤にして、青葉の梢猶あはれ也。卯の花の白妙に、茨の花の咲そひて、雪にもこゆる心地ぞする。古人冠を正し衣装を改し事など、清輔の筆にもとゞめ置れしとぞ。

　　　卯の花をかざしに関の晴着かな　　曾良

Day after day had passed in vague uneasiness, but as we approached the Barrier of Shirakawa I felt myself settling into the spirit of travel. I understood now why the poet had sought means to "tell people in the capital somehow" his feelings on crossing the barrier.[16]

Shirakawa is one of the three famous barriers of the north, a place that has attracted the attention of poets. I felt I could hear the autumn winds and see the crimson leaves mentioned in their poems, and this gave even greater beauty to the green leaves on the boughs before me. The white silk of the verbena joined in blossoming with the white of briar roses, making me feel as if I were crossing the barrier in the snow. Some man of long ago once showed his respect for this barrier by straightening his ceremonial cap and changing to a formal court robe, or so it was recorded by Kiyosuke's pen.[17]

unohana wo	Sprigs of verbena
kazashi ni seki no	Thrust in my cap—such will be
haregi kana	My fancy attire.

Sora

卯の花をかざしに関の晴着かな

Sprigs of verbena
Thrust in my cap—such will be
My fancy attire.

48

〈須賀川〉

とかくして越行まゝに、あぶくま川を渡る。左に会津根高く、右に岩城・相馬・三春の庄、常陸・下野の地をさかひて山つらなる。かげ沼と云所を行に、今日は空曇て物影うつらず。須賀川の駅に等窮といふものを尋て、四、五日とゞめらる。先「白河の関いかにこえつるや」と問。「長途のくるしみ、身心つかれ、且は風景に魂うばゝれ、懐旧に腸を断て、はかばかしう思ひめぐらさず。

　　　風流の初やおくの田植うた

無下にこえんもさすがに」と語れば、脇・第三とつゞけて三巻となしぬ。

　此宿の傍に、大きなる栗の木陰をたのみて、世をいとふ僧有。橡ひろふ太山もかくやと閑に覚られて、ものに書付侍る。其詞、

　　　栗といふ文字は西の木と書て、西方浄土に便ありと、

行基菩薩の一生杖にも柱にも此木を用給ふとかや。

　　　世の人の見付ぬ花や軒の栗

After passing in this manner through the Barrier of Shirakawa, we crossed the Abukuma River. To our left towered Aizune Mountain, to our right were the domains of Iwaki, Sōma and Miharu. A mountain range forms the border between the provinces of Hitachi and Shimotsuke.

Today, when we went by Mirror Marsh, the sky was cloudy and there were no reflections. We visited a man named Tōkyū in the post-town of Sukagawa, and he kept us at his house for four or five days. The first thing Tōkyū asked was, "What were your impressions on crossing the Barrier of Shirakawa?" The hardships of our long journey had exhausted me physically and spiritually, and I had been so captivated by the view, so profoundly moved by memories of the past it awakened, that I had been unable to formulate my thoughts. But, as I mentioned to Tōkyū, it would be a pity if I allowed my crossing to go uncelebrated. I composed this verse:

fūryū no   The true beginnings
hajime ya Oku no   Of poetry—an Oku
taue uta   Rice-planting song.

Second and third verses were added to mine, and eventually we composed three scrolls of linked verse.

Not far from this post-town a monk who had turned his back on the world was living in the shade of a great chestnut tree. The tranquility of the scene made me wonder if Saigyō's "deep mountains where I gather chestnuts" were like this, and I dashed off these words on a scrap of paper:

The character for chestnut is written "west" and "tree," an indication of its connection with the paradise to the west.*18 They say that Gyōgi Bosatsu all through his life used wood from this tree for his walking-stick and the pillars of his house.

yo no hito no   Blossoms unnoticed
mitsukenu hana ya   By people of this world—
noki no kuri   Chestnuts by the eaves.

風流の初やおくの田植うた

The true beginnings
Of poetry—an Oku
Rice-planting song.

〈あさか山〉

　等窮が宅を出て五里計、檜皮の宿を離れてあさか山有。路より近し。此あたり沼多し。かつみ刈比もやゝ近うなれば、いづれの草を花かつみとは云ぞと、人々に尋侍れども、更知人なし。沼を尋、人にとひ、「かつみかつみ」と尋ありきて、日は山の端にかゝりぬ。二本松より右にきれて、黒塚の岩屋一見し、福島に宿る。

〈しのぶの里〉

　あくれば、しのぶもぢ摺の石を尋て、忍ぶのさとに行。遥山陰の小里に石半土に埋てあり。里の童部の来りて教ける、「昔は此山の上に侍しを、往来の人の麦草をあらして、此石を試侍をにくみて、此谷につき落せば、石の面下ざまにふしたり」と云。さもあるべき事にや。

　　早苗とる手もとや昔しのぶ摺

Leaving Tōkyū's house we travelled some ten miles. Once we passed Hiwada, we could see Mount Asaka, right before us and near to the road. There are many marshes in this vicinity. As it was close to the time when the water-oat is harvested, I asked various people which plant was the flowering water-oat, but nobody knew.*[19] What with admiring the marshes and asking people again and again about the water-oat, the sun was already touching the edge of the mountain.

At Nihonmatsu we cut off to the right, and after examining briefly the cave of the Black Mound, continued on to Fukushima, where we spent the night.

The next morning we headed for the village of Shinobu in search of the pattern-rubbing stone. The stone lies half buried in the earth in a little village some distance away shaded by distant mountains. Village children came up and told us, "The stone used to be on top of the mountain in the old days, but people who wanted to rub patterns would trample down the barley going back and forth to the stone. That made the farmers so angry they pushed the stone over into this valley, and it fell face down." That may well have happened.

sanae toru	Deft hands that now pluck
temoto ya mukashi	Seedlings, once you used to press
shinobuzuri	Patterns from the stones.

55

早苗<ruby>さなへ</ruby>とる手もとや昔<ruby>むかし</ruby>しのぶ摺<ruby>ずり</ruby>

Deft hands that now pluck
Seedlings, once you used to press
Patterns from the stones.

月の輪のわたしを越て、瀬の上と云宿に出づ。佐藤庄司が旧跡は、左の山際一里半計に有。飯塚の里鯖野と聞て尋々行に、丸山と云に尋あたる。是庄司が旧館也。麓に大手の跡など、人の教ゆるにまかせて泪を落し、又かたはらの古寺に一家の石碑を残す。中にも二人の嫁がしるし、先哀也。女なれどもかひがひしき名の世に聞えつる物かなと袂をぬらしぬ。堕涙の石碑も遠きにあらず。寺に入て茶を乞へば、爰に義経の太刀・弁慶が笈をとゞめて什物とす。

笈も太刀も五月にかざれ紙幟

五月朔日の事也。

We crossed the river at the Moon Wheel (Tsukinowa) ferry, and arrived at the post-town of Senoue. The old ruins from Satō Shōji's time were about three miles to the left, at the edge of the mountain. I was told that they were at Sabano in Iizuka Village, and went around asking people where that might be. I was finally directed to a place called Maruyama. This was where the remains of Satō Shōji's residence stand. I wept when people told me that what was left of the Great Gate of his castle was to be found at the foot of the mountain. At an old temple nearby the gravestones of the entire family are preserved. Among them, the most affecting are those of two women who married into the Satō family. They were women, but what a reputation for heroism they left behind! At the thought I wetted my sleeve with tears. One need not go to China to find a gravestone that induces tears.

I went into the temple to ask for some tea, only to discover that Yoshitsune's sword and Benkei's portable altar were kept here as temple treasures.

oi mo tachi mo	Sword and altar both
satsuki ni kazare	Display on Boy's Day in May
kaminobori	When paper banners fly.[20]

This took place on the first day of the fifth month.

笠も太刀も五月（さつき）にかざれ紙幟（かみのぼり）

Sword and altar both
Display on Boy's Day in May
When paper banners fly.

〈飯塚〉

　其夜飯塚にとまる。温泉あれば、湯に入て宿をかるに、土坐に筵を敷て、あやしき貧家也。灯もなければ、ゐろりの火かげに寝所をまうけて臥す。夜に入て、雷鳴雨しきりに降て、臥る上よりもり、蚤・蚊にせられて眠らず。持病さへおこりて、消入計になん。短夜の空もやうやう明れば、又旅立ぬ。猶夜の余波、心すゝまず。馬かりて桑折の駅に出る。遥なる行末をかゝえて、斯る病覚束なしといへど、羈旅辺土の行脚、捨身無常の観念、道路にしなん、是天の命なりと、気力聊とり直し、路縦横に踏で伊達の大木戸をこす。

〈笠島〉

　鐙摺、白石の城を過、笠島の郡に入れば、藤中将実方の塚はいづくのほどならんと、人にとへば、「是より遥右に見ゆる山際の里を、みのわ・笠島と云、道祖神の社、かた見の薄、今にあり」と教ゆ。此比の五月雨に道いとあしく、身つかれ侍れば、よそながら眺やりて過るに、簑輪・笠島も五月雨の折にふれたりと、

　　笠島はいづこ五月のぬかり道

岩沼に宿る。

That night we spent at Iizuka. We bathed at the hot springs there, and later went to hire a room at an inn. It proved to be a wretched hovel with straw mats spread on the dirt floor. There weren't even any lanterns, so we made our beds in the light from the hearth fire and lay there. That night the thunder roared, and the rain poured without let-up, leaking onto the place where we lay. I couldn't sleep because I was tormented by fleas and mosquitoes, and to make matters worse, I had an attack of my usual complaint, so severe I almost fainted.

The sky of the short summer night at last grew light, and we resumed our journey. The after-effects of the preceding night lingered on, and I took little pleasure in our travels. We hired horses and pushed on to the post-town of Koori. I felt uneasy over my illness, recalling how far away our destination was, but I reasoned with myself that when I started out on this journey to remote parts of the country it was with an awareness that I was risking my life. Even if I should die on the road, this would be the will of Heaven. These thoughts somewhat restored my spirits, and walking now with greater assurance, I passed by the Great Gate of Date.

We left behind us Abumisuri and the White Stone Castle, then entered the district of Kasashima—Rainhat Island. When I asked a man where the tomb of the Middle Captain Sanekata[21] might be, he answered, "Those villages you can see at the foot of the mountain way off there to the right are Raincoat Wheel and Rainhat Island. You'll find there the shrine to the God of the Road and the "susuki-grass that is my keepsake," mentioned in the poem."[22] The condition of the road had become extremely bad because of the recent rains, and I was also very tired; so I contented myself with gazing at Rainhat Island from the distance. Raincoat Wheel and Rainhat Island are names well suited to the early summer rains, I thought.

Kasajima wa	Rainhat Island—
izuko satsuki no	Where did you say it was?
nukari michi	Muddy roads in May.

We spent the night at Iwanuma.

笠島はいづこ五月のぬかり道

Rainhat Island—
Where did you say it was?
Muddy roads in May.

〈武隈〉

　武隈の松にこそ、め覚る心地はすれ。根は土際より二木にわかれて、昔の姿うしなはずとしらる。先能因法師思ひ出。往昔、むつのかみにて下りし人、此木を伐て名取川の橋杭にせられたる事などあればにや、「松は此たび跡もなし」とは詠たり。代々、あるは伐、あるひは植継などせしと聞に、今将千歳のかたちとゝのほひて、めでたき松のけしきになん侍し。

　「武隈の松みせ申せ遅桜」と、挙白と云ものゝ餞別したりければ、

　　桜より松は二木を三月越し

66

The Pine of Takekuma is truly a startling sight. Its roots divide quite close to the ground into two trunks, proof that it has lost none of its ancient appearance. My first thoughts were of the Abbot Nōin. Many years ago, when a nobleman who had come down from the capital to serve as Governor of Mutsu, he cut down the Pine of Takekuma and used the wood for stakes supporting the bridge over the Natori River. That may be why Nōin wrote in his poem, "No trace is left now of the pine."[23] I was told that in generation after generation the pine has been felled, only to be replaced by another grafted onto the original trunk. It now seems once again to have attained its full splendor of a thousand years, a magnificent sight indeed.

When I set out on my journey Kyohaku presented me with this poem of parting:

Takekuma no	Let him see at least
matsu mise mōse	The pine of Takekuma,
osozakura	Late-blooming cherry.

That is why I now wrote:

sakura yori	Since cherry-blossom time
matsu wa futaki wo	I've pined; now I see a twin pine
mitsukigoshi	Three months afterwards.

桜より松は二木を三月越し<ruby>二<rt>ふた</rt></ruby><ruby>木<rt>き</rt></ruby>を<ruby>三<rt>み</rt></ruby><ruby>月<rt>つき</rt></ruby><ruby>越<rt>ご</rt></ruby>し

Since cherry-blossom time
I've pined; now I see a twin pine
Three months afterwards.

〈宮城野〉

名取川を渡て仙台に入。あやめふく日也。旅宿をもとめて、四、五日逗留す。爰に画工加右衛門と云ものあり。聊心ある者と聞て、知る人になる。この者、年比さだかならぬ名どころを考置侍ればとて、一日案内す。宮城野の萩茂りあひて、秋の気色思ひやらるゝ。玉田・よこ野、つゝじが岡はあせび咲ころ也。日影ももらぬ松の林に入て、爰を木の下と云とぞ。昔もかく露ふかければこそ、「みさぶらひみかさ」とはよみたれ。

薬師堂・天神の御社など拝て、其日はくれぬ。猶、松島・塩がまの所々画に書て送る。且、紺の染緒つけたる草鞋二足餞す。さればこそ、風流のしれもの、爰に至りて其実を顕す。

あやめ草足に結ん草鞋の緒

〈壺の碑〉

かの画図にまかせてたどり行ば、おくの細道の山際に十符の菅有。今も年々十符の菅菰を調て国守に献ずと云り。

　　壺碑　市川村多賀城に有。

つぼの石ぶみは、高サ六尺余、横三尺計歟。苔を穿て文字幽也。四維国界之数里をしるす。「此城、神亀元年、按察使鎮守符将軍大野朝臣東人之所里也。天平宝字六年、参議東海東山節度使、同将軍恵美朝臣獺修造而。十二月朔日」と有。聖武皇帝の御時に当れり。

We crossed the Natori River and entered Sendai. It was the day they celebrate by covering their roofs with irises. We found an inn where we stayed four or five days. A painter named Kaemon lives here. I heard he was a person of some taste, and got to know him. He told me that for years he had been tracing places mentioned in poetry whose whereabouts were now unknown, and he spent a whole day guiding me to them. The fields of Miyagi were thick with clover, and I could imagine how lovely they would look in autumn. This was the season when andromeda blooms in Tamada, in Yokono, and on Azalea Hill. We went into a grove where the pines grew so densely that sunlight could not penetrate. They call this place "Under-the-Trees." It must be because dew was just as heavy in the old days than the poet wrote, "Samurai, tell your lord to take his umbrella!"[24]

We spent one whole day worshipping at the Hall of the Healing Buddha, the Tenjin Shrine, and other holy places. Kaemon presented me with sketches of Matsushima, Shiogama, and other famous places along our route, and with a farewell present of a pair of straw sandals with dark blue cords. These gifts showed him to be a person of exceptional taste.

ayame kusa	I will bind iris
ashi ni musuban	Blossoms round my feet—
waraji no o	Cords for my sandals!

We continued on our way, following a map Kaemon gave us. At the foot of the mountains that border the Narrow Road of Oku, the famous Tō sedge was growing. They say that even now the people of the district present the local daimyo with mats woven of this sedge.

The Tsubo monument[25] stands at Taga Castle in the village of Ichimura. It is over six feet high and about three feet wide, I imagine. When I scraped away the moss covering the stone, an inscription could faintly be seen underneath, recording the distances to all corners of the country. It states: "This castle was built in the first year of Jinki [724] by Ōno asomi Azumabito, Inspector and Governor General, and repaired in the sixth year of Tempyō-hōji [762] by Emi no asomi Asakari, Councillor, Commanding General of the Eastern Sea and the Eastern Mountain districts, and Governor General. First day of the twelfth month."

あやめ草足に結ん草鞋の緒を

I will bind iris
Blossoms round my feet—
Cords for my sandals!

72

むかしよりよみ置る歌枕、おほく語伝ふといへども、山崩川流て道あらたまり、石は埋て土にかくれ、木は老て若木にかはれば、時移り、代変じて、其跡たしかならぬ事のみを、爰に至りて疑なき千歳の記念、今眼前に古人の心を閲す。行脚の一徳、存命の悦び、羈旅の労をわすれて、泪も落るばかり也。

〈末の松山〉

　それより野田の玉川・沖の石を尋ぬ。末の松山は、寺を造て末松山といふ。松のあひあひ皆墓はらにて、はねをかはし枝をつらぬる契の末も、終はかくのごときと、悲しさも増りて、塩がまの浦に入相のかねを聞。

五月雨の空聊はれて、夕月夜幽に、籬が島もほど近し。蜑の小舟こぎつれて、肴わかつ声々に、「つなでかなしも」とよみけん心もしられて、いとゞ哀也。

其夜目盲法師の琵琶をならして、奥上るりと云ものをかたる。平家にもあらず、舞にもあらず、ひなびたる調子うち上て、枕ちかうかしましけれど、さすがに辺土の遺風忘れざるものから、殊勝に覚らる。

Many are the names that have been preserved for us in poetry from ancient times, but mountains crumble and rivers disappear, new roads replace the old, stones are buried and vanish in the earth, trees grow old and give way to saplings. Time passes and the world changes. The remains of the past are shrouded in uncertainty. And yet, here before my eyes was a monument which none would deny had lasted a thousand years. I felt as though I were looking into the minds of the men of old. "This," I thought, "is one of the pleasures of travel and of living to be old." I forgot the weariness of my journey and was moved to tears by my joy.

We next visited the Tama River of Noda, and Rock-off-the-Shore, places known from poetry. On the mountain called Pine-to-the-End there is a temple with the same name.[26] When I noticed that the ground between the pines was filled with graves, I was overcome with sadness at the thought that even the most enduring pledge of devotion between husband and wife must come to this. Then, as I reached the Bay of Shiogama, I heard the vesper bell toll its message of evanescence.

The sky had cleared a little after a steady rain. Under the faintly shining evening moon the island of Magaki across the water seemed close enough to touch. Little fishing boats were being rowed towards the shore, and I could hear the voices of the fishermen as they divided up the catch. I thought to myself with pleasure, "Now at last I understand why the poet wrote,

Michinoku wa	In Michinoku
izuku wa aredo	Every place has its charm,
Shiogama no	But Shiogama,
ura kogu fune no	When rowboats are pulled to shore
tsunade kanashimo	Is most wonderful of all.[27]

That night I listened to a blind magician play the biwa and chant north-country ballads. They were quite unlike the usual war tales or the dance-songs.[28] The sound of his high-pitched countrified voice close to my pillow was distressing, but it gave me special satisfaction to think that the traditional way of reciting the old ballads had not been forgotten in this remote place.

〈塩 竈〉

早朝、塩がまの明神に詣。国守再興せられて、宮柱ふとしく、彩椽き
らびやかに、石の階九仭に重り、朝日あけの玉がきをかゝやかす。かゝ
る道の果、塵土の境まで、神霊あらたにましますこそ、吾国の風俗なれ
と、いと貴けれ。神前に古き宝燈有。かねの戸びらの面に、「文治三年
和泉三郎奇進」と有。五百年来の俤、今目の前にうかびて、そゞろに珍
し。渠は勇義忠孝の士也。佳命今に至りて、したはずといふ事なし。誠
「人能道を勤、義を守べし。名もまた是にしたがふ」と云り。日既午に
ちかし。船をかりて松島にわたる。其間二里余、雄島の磯につく。

Early the next morning we visited the Myōjin Shrine in Shiogama. As rebuilt by the governor of the province, the shrine has imposing pillars, brightly painted rafters, and flight upon flight of stone steps. The morning sun was shining brightly on the vermilion lacquered fence around the shrine. I was profoundly impressed to think that it was typical of our country for the miraculous manifestation of the gods to have occurred in so distant a place, at the very end of the world.

Before the shrine is an old lantern. A metal door bears the inscription, "Presented by Izumi Saburō in the third year of Bunji [1187]." It was strange how these words evoked scenes of five hundred years ago. Izumi was a brave and loyal warrior whose fame has lasted to the present; there is no one who does not hold him in esteem. It has been truly said: "A man should practice the way and maintain his righteousness. Fame will follow of itself."[*29]

It was already close to noon. We hired a boat and crossed to Matsushima. After another five miles on the water we arrived at the beach of the island of Ojima.

〈松 島〉

抑ことふりにたれど、松島は扶桑第一の好風にして、凡洞庭・西湖を恥ず。東南より海を入て、江の中三里、浙江の潮をたゝふ。島々の数を尽して、欹ものは天を指、ふすものは波に匍匐。あるは二重にかさなり、三重に畳みて、左にわかれ右につらなる。負るあり抱るあり、児孫愛すがごとし。松の緑こまやかに、枝葉汐風に吹たはめて、屈曲をのづからためたるがごとし。其気色窅然として、美人の顔を粧ふ。ちはや振神のむかし、大山ずみのなせるわざにや。造化の天工、いづれの人か筆をふるひ詞を尽さむ。

雄島が磯は地つゞきて海に出たる島也。雲居禅師の別室の跡、坐禅石など有。将、松の木陰に世をいとふ人も稀々見え侍りて、落穂・松笠など打けふりたる草の菴閑に住なし、いかなる人とはしられずながら、先なつかしく立寄ほどに、月海にうつりて、昼のながめ又あらたむ。江上に帰りて宿を求れば、窓をひらき二階を作て、風雲の中に旅寝するこそ、あやしきまで妙なる心地はせらるれ。

松島や鶴に身をかれほとゝぎす　　　曾良

予は口をとぢて眠らんとしていねられず。旧庵をわかるゝ時、素堂、松島の詩あり。原安適、松がうらしまの和歌を贈らる。袋を解て、このひの友とす。且、杉風・濁子が発句あり。

No matter how often it has been said, it is nonetheless true that the scenery at Matsushima is the finest in Japan, in no way inferior to T'ung-t'ing or the Western Lake in China. The sea flows in from the southeast forming a bay seven miles across, and the incoming tide surges in massively, just as in Che-chiang. There are countless islands. Some rise up and point at the sky; the low-lying ones crawl into the waves. There are islands piled double or even stacked three high. To the left the islands stand apart; to the right they are linked together. Some look as if they carried little islands on their backs, others as if they held the islands in their arms, evoking a mother's love of her children. The green of the pines is of a wonderful darkness, and their branches are constantly bent by winds from the sea, so that their crookedness seems to belong to the nature of the trees. The scene has the mysterious charm of the face of a beautiful woman. I wonder if Matsushima was created by the God of the Mountains in the Age of the Gods? What man could capture in a painting or a poem the wonder of this masterpiece of nature?

On Ojima, an island connected to the mainland that thrusts out into the sea, are the remains of the Zen master Ungo's hut, and the rock upon which he used to meditate. I caught glimpses here and there under the pines of priests who had abandoned the world. They live quietly in thatched huts from which even at that moment smoke from the fallen pine needles and cones they use as fuel was rising. I did not know what manner of men they might be, but I felt drawn to them. As I walked in their direction I could see the moon shining on the sea, and the scenery of Matsushima quite unlike what it had been during the day. I returned to the shore and took a room at an inn, a two-story building with open windows looking out over the bay. When I lay down to sleep in the breeze and the clouds, I experienced a feeling of strange pleasure.

Matsushima ya	At Matsushima
tsuru ni mi wo kare	Borrow your plumes from the crane
hototogisu	O nightingales!
	Sora

I lay down without composing a poem, but was too excited to sleep. I recalled that when I left my old cottage I was presented by Sodō with a poem in Chinese about Matsushima, and with a tanka by Hara Anteki on Matsugaura Island. I opened my knapsack and made these poems my companions for the night. There were also hokku by Sampū and Jokushi.

松島や鶴に身をかれほとゝぎす

At Matsushima
Borrow your plumes from the crane
O nightingales!

十一日、瑞岩寺に詣。当寺三十二世の昔、真壁の平四郎出家して入唐、帰朝の後開山す。其後に、雲居禅師の徳化に依て、七堂甍改りて、金壁荘厳光を輝、仏土成就の大伽藍とはなれりける。彼見仏聖の寺はいづくにやとしたはる。

〈石の巻〉

　十二日、平和泉と心ざし、あねはの松・緒だえの橋など聞伝て、人跡稀に雉兎蒭蕘の往かふ道そこともわかず、終に路ふみたがえて、石の巻といふ湊に出。「こがね花咲」とよみて奉たる金花山、海上に見わたし、数百の廻船入江につどひ、人家地をあらそひて、竈の煙立つゞけたり。思ひかけず斯ろ所にも来れる哉と、宿からんとすれど、更に宿かす人なし。漸まどしき小家に一夜をあかして、明れば又しらぬ道まよひ行。袖のわたり・尾ぶちの牧・まのゝ萱はらなどよそめにみて、遥なる堤を行。心細き長沼にそふて、戸伊摩と云所に一宿して、平泉に到る。其間廿余里ほどゝおぼゆ。

On the eleventh we visited the Zuigan Temple. Many years ago, thirty-two generations before the present abbot, Makabe no Heishirō entered Buddhist orders, went to China for study, and founded this temple after his return to Japan. Later, the seven halls of the temple were rebuilt as the result of the virtuous efforts of the Zen monk Ungo. Now the temple has become a great hall of worship, the golden walls shining with a splendor worthy of Buddha's paradise.

I wondered where the temple of the Holy Man Kembutsu might be.

On the twelfth we set out for Hiraizumi by way of the Pine of Anewa and the Bridge of Odae, names familiar from poetry. There was hardly anyone on the road, which was no better than a trail hunters or woodcutters might use. Not knowing where we were, we ended up by taking the wrong way and emerging at a port called Ishinomaki. Far out across the water we could see Kinka Mountain "where bloom the golden flowers."[*30] Hundreds of merchant ships clustered in the bay. In the town the houses fought for space, and smoke rose continuously from hearth fires.

I thought to myself, "I never intended to come anywhere like this…" We looked for lodgings for the night, but were refused by everyone. Finally, we found a wretched little hut where we passed the night. Early the next morning we set out uncertainly on another unfamiliar road. As we travelled over a long embankment we could see in the distance Sleeve-Crossing, the Horse Pastures, the Vine Fields of Mano and other places celebrated in poetry.[*31] We skirted the Long Marsh, a depressing place. We stopped for the night at a town called Toima, and then went on to Hiraizumi. We had covered over fifty miles, I believe.

夏草や兵（つはもの）どもが夢の跡

The summer grasses—
Of brave soldiers' dreams
The aftermath.

<平泉>

三代の栄耀一睡の中にして、大門の跡は一里こなたに有。秀衡が跡は田野に成て、金鶏山のみ形を残す。先高館にのぼれば、北上川南部より流る丶大河也。衣川は和泉が城をめぐりて、高館の下にて大河に落入。泰衡等が旧跡は、衣が関を隔て、南部口をさし堅め、夷をふせぐとみえたり。偖も義臣すぐつて此城にこもり、功名一時の叢となる。「国破れて山河あり、城春にして草青みたり」と、笠打敷て、時のうつるまで泪を落し侍りぬ。

夏草や兵どもが夢の跡

卯の花に兼房みゆる白毛かな　　曾良

兼て耳驚したる二堂開帳す。経堂は三将の像をのこし、光堂は三代の棺を納め、三尊の仏を安置す。七宝散うせて、珠の扉風にやぶれ、金の柱霜雪に朽て、既頽廃空虚の叢と成べきを、四面新に囲て、甍を覆て風雨を凌。暫時千歳の記念とはなれり。

五月雨の降のこしてや光堂

The three generations of glory of the Fujiwara of Hiraizumi vanished in the space of a dream. The ruins of their Great Gate are two miles this side of the castle. Where once Hidehira's mansion stood there are now fields, and only Golden Cockerel Mountain, the artificial hill constructed at his command, retains its old appearance.

We first climbed up to Palace-on-the-Heights, from where we could see the Kitagami, a big river that flows down from Nambu. The Koromo River circles Izumi Saburō's castle, then flows into the big river below Palace-on-the-Heights. The ruins of Yasuhira's time are on the other side of the Koromo Barrier, seemingly to protect the Nambu gateway from intrusion by the Ainu. It was at Palace-on-the-Heights that Yoshitsune and his picked retainers fortified themselves, but his glory turned in a moment into this wilderness of grass. "Countries may fall, but their rivers and mountains remain; when spring comes to the ruined castle, the grass is green again."[32] These lines went through my head as I sat on the ground, my bamboo hat spread under me. There I sat weeping, unaware of the passage of time.

natsukusa ya	The summer grasses—
tsuwamono domo ga	Of brave soldiers' dreams
yume no ato	The aftermath.

unohana ni	In the verbena
Kanefusa miyuru	I seem to see Kanefusa—
shiraga kana	Behold his white hair![33]

Sora

The two halls of the Chūson Temple, whose wonders I had heard of and marvelled at, were both open. The Sutra Hall contains statues of the three generals of Hiraizumi; the Golden Hall has their coffins and an enshrined Buddhist trinity. The "seven precious things" were scattered and lost, the gem-inlaid doors broken by the wind, and the pillars fretted with gold flaked by the frost and snow. The temple would surely have crumbled and turned into an empty expanse of grass had it not been recently strengthened on all sides and the roof tiled to withstand the wind and rain. A monument of a thousand years has been preserved a while longer.

samidare no	Have the rains of spring
furinokoshite ya	Spared you from their onslaught,
hikari-dō	Shining hall of Gold?

蚤虱馬の尿する枕もと

Plagued by fleas and lice,
I hear the horses staling
Right by my pillow.

〈尿前の関〉

　南部道遥にみやりて、岩手の里に泊る。小黒崎・みづの小島を過て、なるごの湯より尿前の関にかゝりて、出羽の国に越んとす。此路旅人稀なる所なれば、関守にあやしめられて、漸として関をこす。大山をのぼつて日既暮ければ、封人の家を見かけて舎を求む。三日風雨あれて、よしなき山中に逗留す。

　　蚤虱馬の尿する枕もと

　あるじの云、是より出羽の国に、大山を隔て、道さだかならざれば、道しるべの人を頼て越べきよしを申。さらばと云て、人を頼侍れば、究竟の若者、反脇指をよこたえ、樫の杖を携て、我々が先に立て行。けふこそ必あやうきめにもあふべき日なれと、辛き思ひをなして後について行。あるじの云にたがはず、高山森々として一鳥声きかず、木の下闇茂りあひて、夜る行がごとし。雲端につちふる心地して、篠の中踏分々々、水をわたり岩に蹴て、肌につめたき汗を流して、最上の庄に出づ。かの案内せしおのこの云やう、「此みち必不用の事有。恙なうをくりまいらせて仕合したり」と、よろこびてわかれぬ。跡に聞てさへ胸とゞろくのみ也。

90

Turning back to look at the road stretching far off to Nambu in the north, we spent the night at the village of Iwade. We passed by Ogurozaki and Mizu no Ojima, and from the hot springs at Narugo headed for Shitomae Barrier, intending to cross into Dewa Province. Travellers are rare along this road, and we were suspiciously examined by guards at the barrier. Only with much trouble did we manage to get through. By the time we had climbed the mountain there, the sun had already set. We found a border guard's house and asked to spend the night. For three days a terrible storm raged, and we had no choice but to remain in those dreary mountains.

nomi shirami	Plagued by fleas and lice,
uma no shito suru	I hear the horses staling
makura moto	Right by my pillow.

Our host told us, "The road from here to Dewa lies through high mountains, and is so badly marked you had best get a guide to show you the way." "Very well," I said, and hired one, a strapping young man who wore a scimitar at his side and carried an oaken stick. He walked ahead of us, and thinking that today we were sure to run into danger, we followed behind. The road was as our host had described it—through densely overgrown high mountains in which not a single bird-cry could be heard. It was dark under the trees, so dark that it was like walking at night. Feeling as though "dust were raining from the edges of the clouds,"[34] we pushed our way through clumps of bamboo-grass, waded across streams, and stumbled against rocks. At last we reached the town of Mogami, our bodies bathed in a cold sweat.

When our guide left us he said happily, "Something unpleasant always happens on this road. I was lucky to have been able to lead you here safely." To hear such words, even after our safe arrival, made our hearts pound.

まゆはきを俤（おもかげ）にして紅粉（べに）の花

They make me recall
A lady's powder puff—
These saffron blossoms.

〈尾花沢〉

　尾花沢にて清風と云者を尋ぬ。かれは富るものなれども志いやしからず。都にも折々かよひて、さすがに旅の情をも知たれば、日比とゞめて、長途のいたはり、さまざまにもてなし侍る。

　　涼しさを我宿にしてねまる也

　　這出よかひやが下のひきの声

　　まゆはきを俤にして紅粉の花

　　蚕飼する人は古代のすがた哉　　　曾良

At Obanazawa I called on Seifū, a man of noble aspirations, despite his riches. He often visits Kyoto, and knows what it feels like to be a traveller. He detained us for several days, showering on us every attention out of sympathy for the hardships we had experienced on our long journey.

suzushisa wo	Making the coolness
wa ga yado ni shite	My abode, here I lie
nemaru nari	Completely at ease.

haiide yo	Come out, come crawling out—
kaiya ga shita no	Underneath the silkworm hut
hiki no koe	The voice of a toad.

mayu haki wo	They make me recall
omokage ni shite	A lady's powder puff—
beni no hana	These saffron blossoms.

kogai suru	The people who tend
hito wa kodai no	The silkworms maintain their
sugata kana	Ancient appearance. Sora

閑さや岩にしみ入蟬の声

How still it is here—
Stinging into the stones,
The locusts' trill.

〈立石寺〉

山形領に立石寺と云山寺あり。慈覚大師の開基にして、殊静閑の地也。一見すべきよし、人々のすゝむるに依て、尾花沢よりとつて返し、其間七里ばかり也。日いまだ暮ず。麓の坊に宿かり置て、山上の堂にのぼる。岩に巌を重て山とし、松栢年旧、土石老て苔滑に、岩上の院々扉を閉て、物の音きこえず。岸をめぐり、岩を這て、仏閣を拝し、佳景寂寞として心すみ行のみおぼゆ。

閑さや岩にしみ入蟬の声

There is a mountain temple in the domain of Yamagata called the Ryūshaku-ji. It was founded by the Great Teacher Jikaku, and is a place noted for its tranquillity. People had urged us to go there "even for a brief look," and we had turned back at Obanazawa to make the journey, a distance of about fifteen miles. It was still daylight when we arrived. After first reserving pilgrim's lodgings at the foot of the mountain, we climbed to the temple itself at the summit. Boulders piled on boulders had created this mountain, and the pines and cedars on its slopes were old. The earth and stones were worn and slippery with moss. At the summit the doors of the temple buildings were all shut, and not a sound could be heard. Circling around the cliffs and crawling over the rocks, we reached the main temple building. In the splendor of the scene and the silence I felt a wonderful peace penetrate my heart.

shizukasa ya	How still it is here—
iwa ni shimiiru	Stinging into the stones,
semi no koe	The locusts' trill.

五月雨をあつめて早し最上川

Gathering seawards
The summer rains, how swift it is!
Mogami River.

〈最上川〉

最上川のらんと、大石田と云所に日和を待。爰に古き誹諧の種こぼれて、忘れぬ花のむかしをしたひ、芦角一声の心をやはらげ、此道にさぐりあしゝて、新古ふた道にふみまよふといへども、みちしるべする人しなければと、わりなき一巻残しぬ。このたびの風流、爰に至れり。

最上川は、みちのくより出て、山形を水上とす。ごてん・はやぶさなど云おそろしき難所有。板敷山の北を流て、果は酒田の海に入。左右山覆ひ、茂みの中に船を下す。是に稲つみたるをや、いな船といふならし。白糸の滝は青葉の隙々に落て、仙人堂、岸に臨て立。水みなぎつて舟あやうし。

五月雨をあつめて早し最上川

We waited for the weather to clear at a place called Ōishida, intending to sail down the Mogami River. People told us that the seeds of the old haikai poetry had been scattered here, and people still recalled nostalgically the unforgotten, long-ago days of its glory; the rustic notes of a reed pipe brought music to their hearts. "We are groping for the right path, uncertain which to follow, the old or the new, but there is no one to guide us on our way," they said, and I had no choice but to compose with them a scroll of poems. The poetry-making of this journey had reached to even such a place.

The Mogami River has its source in Michinoku, and its upper reaches are in Yamagata. The Chessboard and Peregrine Rapids are among the terrifying danger spots in its course. The river flows north of Itajiki Mountain, and finally enters the sea at Sakata. Mountains overhang the river on both sides, and boats are sent downstream through the thick vegetation. Probably what the poet called "rice boats"[35] were boats like mine, except loaded with rice. Through breaks in the green leaves we could see the White Thread Falls. The Hermit's Hall stands facing the riverbank. The river was swollen and the boat in danger.

samidare wo	Gathering seawards
atsumete hayashi	The summer rains, how swift it is!
Mogamigawa	Mogami River.

涼しさやほの三日月の羽黒山

How cool it is here—
A crescent moon faintly hovers
Over Mount Haguro.

〈羽黒〉

六月三日、羽黒山に登る。図司左吉と云者を尋て、別当代会覚阿闍梨に謁す。南谷の別院に舎して、憐愍の情こまやかにあるじせらる。

四日、本坊にをゐて誹諧興行。

有難や雪をかほらす南谷

五日、権現に詣。当山開闢能除大師は、いづれの代の人と云事をしらず。延喜式に「羽州里山の神社」と有。書写、「黒」の字を「里山」となせるにや。羽州黒山を中略して羽黒山と云にや。出羽といへるは、「鳥の羽毛を此国の貢に献る」と風土記に侍とやらん。月山、湯殿を合て三山とす。当寺武江東叡に属して、天台止観の月明らかに、円頓融通の法の灯かゝげそひて、僧坊棟をならべ、修験行法を励し、霊山霊地の験効、人貴且恐る。繁栄長にして、めで度御山と謂つべし。

On the third day of the sixth month we climbed Mount Haguro. We visited there a man named Zushi Sakichi and had an audience with the acting superintendent, the High Priest Egaku. The High Priest put us up at the branch temple in Southern Valley, and showed us the most delicate attentions.

On the fourth there was a haikai gathering in the abbot's living quarters.

arigata ya	So holy a place—
yuki wo kaorasu	The snow itself is scented
minamidani	At Southern Valley.

On the fifth we worshipped the incarnation of the Buddha. I have no idea in what period the founder of this temple, the Great Teacher Nōjo, lived. It says in the *Engishiki*[*36] that there is a Shintō shrine at Satoyama in Dewa Province. I wonder if, when the work was copied, the scribe did not break up the character kuro into sato and yama. Perhaps, too, Haguroyama was a contraction of Ushū Kuroyama.[*37] Apparently the name Dewa ("present feathers") originated in the custom observed in this province of offering feathers in tribute, or so it says in the gazetteer. Haguro, together with Yudono and Moon mountains constitute the Three Mountains of Dewa. The temple here is affiliated with the Eastern Hiei Temple in Edo. The moon of the Tendai "concentration and insight" discipline shines brightly, and the teaching of immediate perfection through identity is a lamp that burns ever more brilliantly. The living quarters of the priests are ranged eaves-to-eaves, and yamabushi practice their austerities zealously. These signs of the miraculous power of this holy site stir reverence and awe. Long has it flourished, this truly wondrous mountain.

雲の峰幾つ崩て月の山

The peaks of clouds
Have crumbled into fragments—
The moonlit mountain!

八日、月山にのぼる。木綿しめ身に引かけ、宝冠に頭を包、強力と云ものに道びかれて、雲霧山気の中に、氷雪を踏てのぼる事八里、更に日月行道の雲関に入かとあやしまれ、息絶身こゞえて頂上に臻れば、日没て月顕る。笹を鋪、篠を枕として、臥て明るを待。日出て雲消れば、湯殿に下る。

On the eighth we climbed Moon Mountain. We slung knotted paper cords around our bodies, and swathed our heads with "sacred crowns."*[38] What they call a "strongman," a porter, led us some fifteen miles through the clouds, mists, and mountain air, over snows that never melt. Would we, I wondered, be passing next through the cloud gate into the courses of the sun and moon? My breath came short, and my body was numbed by the cold. By the time we reached the summit, the sun had set and the moon appeared in the sky. We spread out pallets of bamboo-grass, and with bamboo stalks for our pillows, lay there, waiting for the dawn. When the sun came out the clouds melted away, and we went down to Yudono.

語られぬ湯殿にぬらす袂（たもと）かな

I cannot speak of
Yudono, but see how wet
My sleeve is with tears.

谷の傍に鍛冶小屋と云有。此国の鍛冶、霊水を撰て、爰に潔斎して釼を打、終「月山」と銘を切て世に賞せらる。彼竜泉に釼を淬とかや。干将・莫耶のむかしをしたふ。道に堪能の執あさからぬ事しられたり。岩に腰かけてしばしやすらふほど、三尺ばかりなる桜のつぼみ半ばひらけるあり。ふり積雪の下に埋て、春を忘れぬ遅ざくらの花の心わりなし。炎天の梅花爰にかほるがごとし。行尊僧正の歌の哀も爰に思ひ出て、猶まさりて覚ゆ。惣て、此山中の微細、行者の法式として他言する事を禁ず。仍て筆をとゞめて記さず。坊に帰れば、阿闍梨の需に依て、三山順礼の句々短冊に書。

　　　涼しさやほの三日月の羽黒山

　　　雲の峰幾つ崩て月の山

　　　語られぬ湯殿にぬらす袂かな

　　　湯殿山銭ふむ道の泪かな　　　曾良

Along the sides of the valley there formerly were sword-smiths' huts. The swordsmiths of this province used the holy water from the mountain to purify themselves and temper their blades. At the very last they would incise the name "Moon Mountain" on swords that were prized everywhere. The Chinese, they say, tempered their blades in the Dragon Springs. Their desire to achieve swords of the quality of the ancient Kan-chiang and Mo-yeh*[39] suggests how deep their devotion is to their craft.

As I sat on a rock resting for a while, I noticed a cherry tree, barely three feet high, with buds just opened. To think that even when they were buried under snow drifts these late-blooming cherry blossoms had not forgotten the spring! How charming of them! It was like catching the fragrance of plum blossoms on a burning summer's day. I remembered then the pathos evoked in the poem by the Abbot Gyōson,*[40] but I thought that this tree was even more affecting.

It is forbidden by the rules of the ascetics' order to disclose details of this mountain to other people. I will therefore lay down my pen and write no more.

When I returned to the temple, at the abbot's request I wrote on poem-cards the verses I had composed during my pilgrimage to the three mountains.

suzushisa ya	How cool it is here—
hono mikazuki no	A crescent moon faintly hovers
Haguro san	Over Mount Haguro.

kumo no mine	The peaks of clouds
ikutsu kuzurete	Have crumbled into fragments—
tsuki no yama	The moonlit mountain!

katararenu	I cannot speak of
Yudono ni nurasu	Yudono, but see how wet
tamoto kana	My sleeve is with tears.

Yudono san	Yudono Mountain—
zeni fumu michi no	As I tread on pilgrims' coins,
namida kana	Behold these my tears. Sora

暑き日を海にいれたり最上川

The burning sun
It has washed into the sea—
Mogami River.

羽黒を立て、鶴が岡の城下、長山氏重行と云物のふの家にむかへられて、誹諧一巻有。左吉も共に送りぬ。川舟に乗て、酒田の湊に下る。淵庵不玉と云医師の許を宿とす。

　　　あつみ山や吹浦かけて夕すゞみ

　　　暑き日を海にいれたり最上川

We left Haguro and continued our journey to the castle town of Tsurugaoka where we were guests of a samurai named Nagayama Shigeyuki. We composed a scroll of linked-verse at his house. Sakichi accompanied us all the way. We boarded a river boat and went down to the port of Sakata. We stayed at the house of a physician named En'an Fugyoku.

atsumi yama ya	From Hot Springs Mountain
Fukuura kakete	All the way to Blowing Bay—
yūsuzumi	The cool of evening.

atsuki hi wo	The burning sun
umi ni iretari	It has washed into the sea—
Mogamigawa	Mogami River.

象潟や雨に西施(せいし)がねぶの花

Kisakata—
Seishi sleeping in the rain,
Wet mimosa blossoms.

〈象潟〉

　江山水陸の風光数を尽して、今象潟に方寸を責。酒田の湊より東北の方、山を越、礒を伝ひ、いさごをふみて其際十里、日影やゝかたぶく比、汐風真砂を吹上、雨朦朧として鳥海の山かくる。闇中に莫作して「雨も又奇也」とせば、雨後の晴色又頼母敷と、蜑の苫屋に膝をいれて、雨の晴を待。其朝天能霽て、朝日花やかにさし出る程に、象潟に舟をうかぶ。先能因島に舟をよせて、三年幽居の跡をとぶらひ、むかふの岸に舟をあがれば、「花の上こぐ」とよまれし桜の老木、西行法師の記念をのこす。

　江上に御陵あり。神功后宮の御墓と云。寺を干満珠寺と云。此処に行幸ありし事いまだ聞ず。いかなる事にや。此寺の方丈に座して簾を捲ば、風景一眼の中に尽て、南に鳥海、天をさゝえ、其陰うつりて江にあり。西はむやむやの関、路をかぎり、東に堤を築て、秋田にかよふ道遥に、海北にかまえて、浪打入る所を汐こしと云。江の縦横一里ばかり、俤松島にかよひて、又異なり。松島は笑ふが如く、象潟はうらむがごとし。寂しさに悲しみをくはえて、地勢魂をなやますに似たり。

After having seen so many splendid views of both land and sea, I could think of nothing now but Kisakata. We journeyed to the northeast from the port of Sakata, climbing over hills, following along the shore, plodding through the sand, a distance of about twenty miles in all. As the sun was sinking in the sky a breeze from the sea stirred up the sand, and a misty rain started to fall, obscuring Chōkai Mountain. We groped ahead in the darkness. I felt sure that if Kisakata was exquisite in the rain, it would prove no less wonderful when it cleared. We squeezed into a fisherman's thatch-covered hut and waited for the rain to stop.

The next morning the weather cleared beautifully. When the morning sun rose in all its splendor, we took a boat out on the lagoon of Kisakata. We put in first at Nōin Island, where we visited the remains of the hut in which Nōin lived in seclusion for three years. On the opposite shore, when we landed from our boat, we saw the old cherry tree that stands as a memento of Saigyō, who wrote of it:

Kisakata	At Kisakata
sakura wa nami ni	A cherry tree is covered
uzumorete	At times by the waves;
hana no ue kogu	Fishermen must row their boats
ama no tsuribune	Above the cherry blossoms.

Near the water is a tomb they say is the Empress Jingū's, and the temple standing nearby is called the Ebb-and-Flow-Pearls Temple.[41] I had never before heard that the Empress had come this way. I wonder if it is true.

Seated within the priests' quarters of the temple, I rolled up the bamboo blinds and took in all at once the whole spectacle of Kisakata. To the south loomed Mount Chōkai, supporting the heavens; its image was reflected in the water. To the west, one can see as far as Muyamuya Barrier; to the east, the road over the embankment leads to Akita in the distance. The sea is to the north. The place where the waves of the sea break into the lagoon is called Tide-Crossing. Kisakata is about two miles in either direction.

Kisakata resembles Matsushima, but there is a difference. Matsushima seems to be smiling, but Kisakata wears a look of grief. There is a sadness mingled with the silent calm, a configuration to trouble the soul.

象潟や雨に西施がねぶの花

汐越や鶴はぎぬれて海涼し

　　祭礼

象潟や料理何くふ神祭　　　曾良
蜑の家や戸板を敷て夕涼　　　みのゝ国の商人　低耳

　　　岩上に睢鳩の巣をみる

波こえぬ契ありてやみさごの巣　　　曾良

Kisakata ya
ame ni Seishi ga
nebu no hana

Kisakata—
Seishi sleeping in the rain,[42]
Wet mimosa blossoms.

Shiogoshi ya
tsuru hagi nurete
umi suzushi

Tide-Crossing—
The crane's long legs are wetted
How cool the sea is!

Festival[43]

Kisakata ya
ryōri nani kuu
kami matsuri

Kisakata—
What special food do they eat
At the festival?

Sora[44]

ama no ya ya
toita wo shikite
yūsuzumi

A fisherman's hut—
Laying out their doors, they enjoy
The cool of evening.

Teiji[45]

On seeing an osprey's nest on a rock

nami koenu
chigiri arite ya
misago no su

Did they vow never
To part till waves topped their rock?
The nest of the ospreys.

Sora

〈越後路〉

　酒田の余波日を重て、北陸道の雲に望。遥々のおもひ胸をいたましめ
て、加賀の府まで百卅里と聞。鼠の関をこゆれば、越後の地に歩行を改
て、越中の国一ぶりの関に到る。此間九日、暑湿の労に神をなやまし、
病おこりて事をしるさず。

　　文月や六日も常の夜には似ず

　　荒海や佐渡によこたふ天河

I was so loath to leave Sakata that the days there piled up, but now I turned my gaze to the distant clouds of Hokuriku. The thought of another long journey filled me with anxiety. I was told that the distance to Kanazawa, the capital of Kaga Province, is over three hundred miles.

Once past the Barrier of Nezu, we were in Echigo Province. We pursued our journey as far as the Barrier of Ichifuri in Etchū. During these nine days of travel I was worn out and depressed by the heat and the rain. I had a bout of illness and wrote nothing.

fumizuki ya	The seventh month—
muika mo tsune no	Even the sixth does not seem,
yo ni wa nizu	Like a usual night.[46]

araumi ya	Turbulent the sea—
Sado ni yokotau	Across to Sado stretches
ama no kawa	The Milky Way.

荒海や佐渡によこたふ天河

Turbulent the sea—
Across to Sado stretches
The Milky Way.

今日は親しらず・子しらず・犬もどり・駒返しなど云北国一の難所を越てつかれ侍れば、枕引よせて寐たるに、一間隔て面の方に、若き女の声二人計ときこゆ。年老たるおのこの声も交て物語するをきけば、越後の国新潟と云所の遊女成し。伊勢参宮するとて、此関までおのこの送りて、あすは古郷にかへす文したゝめて、はかなき言伝などしやる也。白浪のよする汀に身をはふらかし、あまのこの世をあさましう下りて、定めなき契、日々の業因、いかにつたなしと、物云をきくきく寐入りて、あした旅立に、我々にむかひて、「行衛しらぬ旅路のうさ、あまり覚束なう悲しく侍れば、見えがくれにも御跡をしたひ侍ん。衣の上の御情に大慈のめぐみをたれて結縁せさせ給へ」と、泪を落す。不便の事には侍れども、「我々は所々にてとゞまる方おほし。只人の行にまかせて行べし。神明の加護、かならず恙なかるべし」と、云捨て出つゝ、哀さしばらくやまざりけらし。

一家に遊女もねたり萩と月

曾良にかたれば、書とゞめ侍る。

130

Today we passed through the most dangerous places in the north country, known as "Parents Forget Their Children," "Children Forget Their Parents," "Dogs Turn Back," and "Horses Return."[*47] I was so exhausted that I drew my pillow to me and lay down as soon as we reached an inn. I could hear the voices of young women, probably two of them, talking in a room one removed from ours at the front of the house. The voice of an old man also took part in the conversation. I gathered from what they were saying that the women were prostitutes from Niigata in Echigo Province. They were on their way to worship at the shrine in Ise, and the man had escorted them here, as far as the Barrier of Ichifuri. They would be sending him back the next day, and they were giving him letters they had written and trivial little messages to take back with him.

"We have wandered over the shores washed by the white waves. Like fisherwomen, we have dived to the depths of this world. What terrible karma accounts for our inconstant vows, the sins we have daily committed? We are wretched indeed..." These were the last words I heard before falling asleep.

The next morning, when we were about to start out, the two women approached us, saying, "We feel so uneasy and depressed at the thought of the difficulties that may await us on the way to an unfamiliar place that we would like to follow behind you, even if out of sight. Grant us this great favor, you who wear the habit of priests, and help us to attain the way of the Buddha." They were in tears.

I answered, "I feel sorry for you, but we must stop at a great many places. You'd better go along with some ordinary travellers. You will be under the protection of the gods. I am sure no harm will come to you." These were my parting words, but for a time I could not shake off my pity for them.

hitotsu ya ni	Under the same roof
yūjo mo netari	Prostitutes were sleeping—
hagi to tsuki	The moon and clover.

I mentioned to Sora what I had composed, and he wrote it down.

一家に遊女もねたり萩と月

Under the same roof
Prostitutes were sleeping—
The moon and clover.

〈那古の浦〉

　くろべ四十八が瀬とかや、数しらぬ川をわたりて、那古と云浦に出。担籠の藤浪は、春ならずとも初秋の哀とふべきものをと、人に尋れば、「是より五里、いそ伝ひして、むかふの山陰にいり、蜑の苫ぶきかすかなれば、蘆の一夜の宿かすものあるまじ」といひをどされて、かゞの国に入。

　　　　早稲の香や分入右は有磯海

People speak of the "forty-eight shallows of the Kurobe," and we did indeed cross many streams before we reached the Inlet of Nako. It was not spring when "the waves of wisteria" at Tako are in bloom, but people urged us to experience the pathos of early autumn there. I asked a man the way, and he replied, "If you follow the shore for about ten miles, you'll find Tako behind yonder mountain. There's nothing there but some miserable thatch-covered fishermen's huts. I doubt very much if you'll find anyone to put you up for the night." Frightened away by his remarks, we continued on to Kaga.

wase no ka ya	Sweet-smelling rice fields!
wakeiru migi wa	To our right as we push through,
Ariso umi	The Ariso Sea.

早稲の香や分入右は有磯海

Sweet-smelling rice fields!
To our right as we push through,
The Ariso Sea.

〈金沢〉

卯の花山・くりからが谷をこえて、金沢は七月中の五日也。爰に大坂よりかよふ商人何処と云者有。それが旅宿をともにす。一笑と云ものは、此道にすける名のほのぼの聞えて、世に知人も侍しに、去年の冬、早世したりとて、其兄追善を催すに、

　　　　塚も動け我泣声は秋の風

　　　　　ある草庵にいざなはれて

　　　　秋涼し手毎にむけや瓜茄子

　　　　　途中吟

　　　　あかあかと日は難面もあきの風

After crossing Verbena Mountain and the Valley of Kurikara, we reached Kanazawa on the fifteenth of the seventh month. We shared lodgings with a merchant named Kasho from Ōzaka.

I had heard vague reports of one Isshō, a man devoted to our art, who had established something of a reputation; but he had died young in the winter of the previous year. On the occasion of a memorial service offered by his elder brother, I wrote:

tsuka mo ugoke   Shake your tomb, reply!
wa ga naku koe wa   My voice that weeps for you
aki no kaze   Is the autumn wind.

On being invited to a thatched hut:

aki suzushi   The cool of autumn—
tegoto ni muke ya   Every hand start peeling
uri nasubi   Melons and eggplants!

On the road:

aka aka to   Redly, redly
hi wa tsurenaku mo The sun shines heartlessly, but
aki no kaze   The wind is autumnal.

あかあかと日は難面<ruby>面<rt>つれなく</rt></ruby>もあきの風

Redly, redly
The sun shines heartlessly, but
The wind is autumnal.

〈小松〉

小松と云所にて

しほらしき名や小松吹萩すゝき

此所、太田の神社に詣。実盛が甲・錦の切あり。往昔、源氏に属せし時、義朝公より給はらせ給とかや。げにも、平士のものにあらず。目庇より吹返しまで、菊から草のほりもの金をちりばめ、竜頭に鍬形打たり。真盛討死の後、木曾義仲願状にそへて、此社にこめられ侍よし、樋口の次郎が使せし事共、まのあたり縁起にみえたり。

むざんやな甲の下のきりぎりす

At a place called Komatsu—Little Pines:

shiorashiki	What a charming name!
na ya komatsu fuku	The wind blows through little pines,
hagi susuki	Clover and susuki.

We went to worship at the Tada Shrine in Komatsu. Sanemori's helmet and fragments of his brocade robe are preserved here. I was told that long ago, while he was serving the Minamoto clan, he received these gifts from Yoritomo. Indeed, these are no ordinary samurai's possessions. The helmet is engraved with a chrysanthemum arabesque pattern inlaid with gold from the frontlet to the aventail, and there are projecting horns on the dragon crest. I gather that Kiso Yoshinaka, after killing Sanemori in battle, offered the helmet to the shrine, together with his prayers for victory. The account of how Higuchi no Jirō, as Yoshinaka's envoy, brought these offerings here is vividly described in the shrine records.

muzan ya na	Alas for mortality!
kabuto no shita no	Underneath the helmet
kirigirisu	A grasshopper.

むざんやな甲<ruby>甲<rt>かぶと</rt></ruby>の下のきりぐす

Alas for mortality!
Underneath the helmet
A grasshopper.

〈那谷〉

　山中の温泉に行ほど、白根が嶽跡にみなしてあゆむ。左の山際に観音堂あり。花山の法皇、三十三所の順礼とげさせ給ひて後、大慈大悲の像を安置し給ひて、那谷と名付給ふと也。那智・谷汲の二字をわかち侍しとぞ。奇石さまざまに、古松植ならべて、萱ぶきの小堂、岩の上に造りかけて、殊勝の土地也。

　　　石山の石より白し秋の風

As we walked along the road to the Yamanaka Hot Springs, we could see over our shoulders the peak of Shirane. To our left, at the foot of a mountain, there was a temple dedicated to Kannon. Long ago, when the cloistered emperor Kazan completed his pilgrimage to the Thirty-Three Temples of Kannon, he installed here a statue of the All-Compassionate, All-Merciful Kannon, and bestowed on the temple the name Nata, combining the na of Nachi and the ta of Tanigumi.[48] A row of ancient pines grows upon the curious rocks of various shapes, and a little rush-covered building stands atop a great boulder. It is a place of marvellous beauty.

Ishiyama no	Whiter, whiter than
ishi yori shiroshi	The stones of Stone Mountain—
aki no kaze	The autumnal wind.[49]

石山の石より白し秋の風

Whiter, whiter than
The stones of Stone Mountain—
The autumnal wind.

〈山中〉

温泉に浴す。基功有明に次と云。

山中や菊はたおらぬ湯の匂

あるじとする物は、久米之助とて、いまだ小童也。かれが父誹諧を好み、洛の貞室、若輩のむかし、爰に来りし比、風雅に辱しめられて、洛に帰て貞徳の門人となつて世にしらる。功名の後、此一村判詞の料を請ずと云。今更むかし語とはなりぬ。

We bathed in the hot springs, which are reputed to be second in their efficacy only to those of Arima.

yamanaka ya   At Yamanaka
kiku wa taoranu   No need to pick chrysanthemums—
yu no nioi   The scent of hot springs.[50]

The innkeeper, Kumenosuke by name, was still a boy. His father had been fond of haikai and once, long ago, when Teishitsu,[51] then a young man, came here from Kyōto, he was quite put to shame by the father's superior knowledge of the art. When he returned to Kyōto, Teishitsu studied under Teitoku and later gained recognition. They say that even after he had become famous he used to correct free of charge verses composed by people of this village. But these are now tales of long ago.

山中や菊はたおらぬ湯の匂

At Yamanaka
No need to pick chrysanthemums—
The scent of hot springs.

曾良は腹を病て、伊勢の国長島と云所にゆかりあれば、先立て行に、

　　　行々てたふれ伏とも萩の原　　　曾良

と書置たり。行もの、悲しみ、残もの、うらみ、隻鳧のわかれて雲にまよふがごとし。予も又、

　　　今日よりや書付消さん笠の露

Sora, having developed stomach trouble, went on ahead to Nagashima in Ise Province where he has relatives. He left this verse for me:

yuki yukite   On, on I travel;
taorefusu tomo   Though I fall and die, let it be
hagi no hara   In fields of clover.

The grief of the one who went ahead, the regret of the one who remained behind—we were like two wild ducks parting and losing their way in the clouds. I too wrote a verse:

kyō yori ya   Today I shall wipe out
kakitsuke kesan   The words written in my hat
kasa no tsuyu   With the dew of tears.[52]

今日よりや書付消さん笠の露

けふ かきつけ かさ

Today I shall wipe out
The words written in my hat
With the dew of tears.

〈全昌寺・汐越の松〉

大聖持の城外、全昌寺といふ寺にとまる。猶加賀の地也。曾良も前の夜、此寺に泊て、

　　　　終宵秋風聞やうらの山

と残す。一夜の隔千里に同じ。吾も秋風を聞て衆寮に臥ば、明ぼのゝ空近う読経声すむまゝに、鐘板鳴て食堂に入。けふは越前の国へと、心早卒にして堂下に下るを、若き僧ども紙・硯をかゝえ、階のもとまで追来る。折節庭中の柳散れば、

　　　　庭掃て出ばや寺に散柳

とりあへぬさまして、草鞋ながら書捨つ。
　越前の境、吉崎の入江を舟に棹して、汐越の松を尋ぬ。

　　　終宵嵐に波をはこばせて

　　　　月をたれたる汐越の松　　　西行

此一首にて数景尽たり。もし一弁を加るものは、無用の指を立るがごとし。

I stayed at a temple called Zenshō-ji on the outskirts of the castle town of Daishōji. This is still in Kaga Province. Sora had spent the previous night at the same temple and left this poem for me:

yo mo sugara	All through the night
akikaze kiku ya	I listened to the autumn wind
ura no yama	In the hills behind.

Though but a single night separated us, it was as if by a thousand miles. That night I too lay sleepless in the priests' study hall listening to the autumn wind. As dawn approached, the sound of voices chanting a sutra reached me clearly. I heard a gong strike and went to the refectory. "Today I must be on my way to Echizen," I was thinking as I hurried down the stairs from the hall, eager to get started. Just then young priests with paper and inkstones in their hands came running after me to the foot of the staircase. The willow in the temple garden was shedding its leaves, so I wrote:

niwa hakite	I'll sweep the garden
idebaya tera ni	Before I leave—in the temple
chiru yanagi	The willow-leaves fall.

I quickly jotted down this impromptu verse, standing in my travel sandals, and then was off.

My boat was poled across Yoshizaki Inlet, the border of Echizen Province. I visited the Tide-Crossing Pines.

yo mo sugara	All through the night
arashi ni nami wo	The waves were driven by a storm
hakobasete	That brought them shoreward;
tsuki wo taretaru	The moon shone suspended from
Shiogoshi no matsu	The pines of Shiogoshi.

In this poem Saigyō said everything that could be said about the various sights. If one attempted to add a single word, it would be as futile as putting an extra finger on a man's hand.

庭掃(は)て出(い)ばや寺に散(ち)柳

I'll sweep the garden
Before I leave—in the temple
The willow-leaves fall.

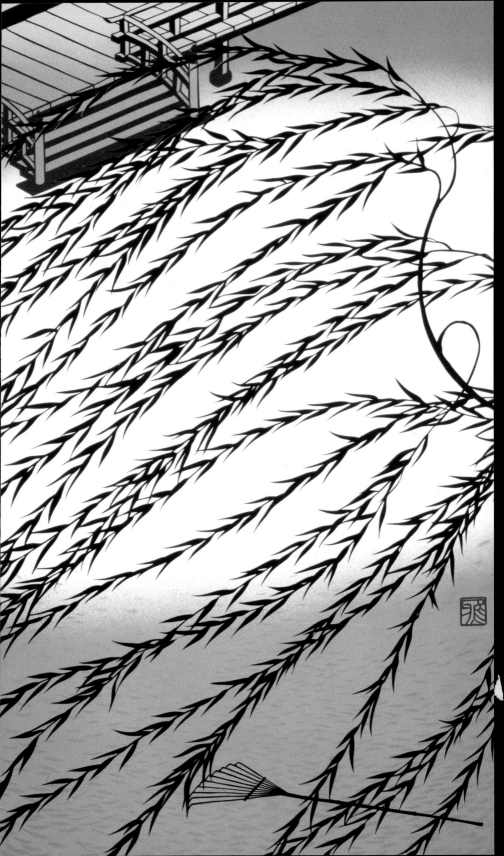

〈天竜寺・永平寺〉

丸岡天竜寺の長老、古き因あれば尋ぬ。又、金沢の北枝といふもの、かりそめに見送りて此処までしたひ来る。所々の風景過さず思ひつゞけて、折節あはれなる作意など聞ゆ。今既別に望みて、

物書て扇引さく余波哉

五十丁山に入て、永平寺を礼す。道元禅師の御寺也。邦機千里を避て、かゝる山陰に跡をのこし給ふも、貴きゆへ有とかや。

〈等 栽〉

福井は三里計なれば、夕飯したゝめて出るに、たそかれの路たどたどし。爰に等栽と云古き隠士有。いづれの年にか、江戸に来りて予を尋遥十とせ余り也。いかに老さらぼひて有にや、将死けるにやと人に尋侍れば、いまだ存命して、そこそこと教ゆ。市中ひそかに引入て、あやしの小家に、夕貌・へちまのはえかゝりて、鶏頭・はゝ木ゞに戸ほそをかくす。さては、此うちにこそと門を扣ば、侘しげなる女の出て、「いづくよりわたり給ふ道心の御坊にや。あるじは此あたり何がしと云ものゝ方に行ぬ。もし用あらば尋給へ」といふ。かれが妻なるべしとしらる。むかし物がたりにこそ、かゝる風情は侍れと、やがて尋あひて、その家に二夜とまりて、名月はつるがのみなとにとたび立。等栽も共に送らんと、裾おかしうからげて、路の枝折とうかれ立。

162

At Maruoka I called on the abbot of the Tenryū Temple, an old acquaintance. A man named Hokushi from Kanazawa, who had intended merely to see me off, acompanied me all the way here. He let no sight of the journey go unnoticed, but wrote verses, some of them quite interesting, about everything we passed. When we were about to say goodby, I wrote:

mono kakite	I scribbled something,
ōgi hikisaku	Planning to tear up my fan—
nagori kana	But parting was sad![53]

I went some three or four miles into the mountains to worship at the Eihei-ji. This was the temple of the Zen master Dōgen. I gather he had some profound reason for leaving the region of the capital and going a thousand leagues to build his temple in mountains such as these.

Fukui was only six or seven miles away, so I set out after supper, walking uncertainly along the twilit road. Fukui is where Tōsai has long lived as a recluse. Once—in what year was it, I wonder?—he came to Edo and called on me. It must have been well over ten years ago. I thought how old and decrepit Tōsai would now be, or perhaps he was even dead. I asked someone about him, and was informed he was still living and his house was in such-and-such a place. Tōsai's shabby little house was buried in an out-of-the-way corner of the town. Moonflowers and bottle-gourds crept over the walls, and cockscomb and broom-grass grew so high they hid his door. "This must be the place," I thought, and knocked on the gate. A poorly dressed woman emerged and asked, "Where have you come from on your pilgrimage, your reverence? The master has gone to visit a gentleman in the vicinity. If you have business with him, please look for him there." I gathered she must be his wife. I thought, "This is just like a scene from that old novel,"[54] and went off in search of Tōsai. I found him without trouble, and spent two nights in his house. Then I set out to see the harvest moon at the Bay of Tsuruga. Tōsai, offering to guide me, tucked up the skirts of his kimono in a comical way. "I'll show you the way!" he declared in high spirits.

物書<ruby>きき<rt></rt></ruby>て扇引さく余波哉

物書<ruby>書<rt>かき</rt></ruby>て扇<ruby>引<rt>あふぎひき</rt></ruby>さく余<ruby>波<rt>なごり</rt></ruby>哉<ruby><rt>かな</rt></ruby>

I scribbled something,
Planning to tear up my fan—
But parting was sad!

　漸白根が嶽かくれて、比那が嶽あらはる。あさむづの橋をわたりて、玉江の蘆は穂に出にけり。鶯の関を過て、湯尾峠を越れば、燧が城、かへるやまに初鴈を聞て、十四日の夕ぐれ、つるがの津に宿をもとむ。

　その夜、月殊晴たり。「あすの夜もかくあるべきにや」といへば、「越路の習ひ、猶明夜の陰晴はかりがたし」と、あるじに酒すゝめられて、けいの明神に夜参す。仲哀天皇の御廟也。社頭神さびて、松の木の間に月のもり入たる、おまへの白砂霜を敷るがごとし。往昔、遊行二世の上人、大願発起の事ありて、みづから草を刈、土石を荷ひ、泥淳をかはかせて、参詣往来の煩なし。古例今にたえず、神前に真砂を荷ひ給ふ。「これを遊行の砂持と申侍る」と、亭主のかたりける。

　　　　月清し遊行のもてる砂の上

　十五日、亭主の詞にたがはず雨降。

　　　　名月や北国日和定なき

Shirane Mountain gradually disappeared from sight, and I saw instead the peak of Hina. I crossed Asamutsu Bridge, and at Tamae saw that the rushes had gone to seed. Passing through the Barrier of Song Birds and over Yunō Pass, we came to Hiuchi Castle. At Kaeru Mountain I heard the cries of the first wild geese of autumn. On the fourteenth I found lodgings at the port of Tsuruga. The moon was particularly bright that night. I asked the innkeeper, "Will it be like this tomorrow night for the full moon?" He replied, "It's hard to guess from one night to the next in Koshiji whether it'll be rainy or fair."

After accepting the sake pressed on me by the innkeeper, I went to the Kei Shrine for night worship. The shrine contains the tomb of the Emperor Chūai. The precincts of the shrine have sanctity, and in the moonlight that filtered through the pines the white sand before the shrine looked as though it were covered with frost. The innkeeper told me, "Once, long ago, the second Pilgrim-Priest asked some great favor of the gods. He himself cut grass and carried earth and stones to dry up the muddy grounds of the shrine. He made it easier in this way for all to come and worship.'[55] This custom has not died out. Priests still carry fine sand to sprinkle before the shrine, calling it the "sand-carrying of the Pilgrim-Priest."

tsuki kiyoshi	How pure the moonlight
yugyō no moteru	On the sand before the shrine
suna no ue	Brought by Pilgrim-Priests.

On the fifteenth, just as the innkeeper had intimated, it rained.

meigetsu ya	Night of the full moon!
hokkoku hiyori	The weather in the north land
sadame naki	Is so uncertain.

月清し遊行のもてる砂の上

How pure the moonlight
On the sand before the shrine
Brought by Pilgrim-Priests.

〈種の浜〉

　十六日、空霽たれば、ますほの小貝ひろはんと、種の浜に舟を走す。海上七里あり。天屋何某と云もの、破籠・小竹筒などこまやかにしたゝめさせ、僕あまた舟にとりのせて、追風時のまに吹着ぬ。浜はわづかなる海士の小家にて、侘しき法花寺あり。爰に茶を飲、酒をあたゝめて、夕ぐれのさびしさ、感に堪たり。

　　寂しさや須磨にかちたる浜の秋

　　浪の間や小貝にまじる萩の塵

其日のあらまし、等栽に筆をとらせて寺に残す。

On the sixteenth the skies cleared and I went by boat to Iro Beach to gather the little masuo shells. The distance over the water was some fifteen miles. My host, a man called Ten'ya, had made elaborate preparations—lunch boxes and bamboo containers filled with sake—and there were a great many servants aboard to wait on us. A fair wind blew us in no time to our destination. On the beach were a few fishermen's huts and a forlorn Nichiren temple where we drank tea and hot sake. The loneliness at dust was overpowering.

sabishisa ya	How lonely it is!
Suma ni kachitaru	Even lonelier than Suma,
hama no aki	Autumn at this beach.
nami no ma ya	What do the waves bring?
kogai ni majiru	Mixed in with little shells,
hagi no chiri	Bits of clover blooms.

I asked Tōsai to write down a summary of what had happened that day and left it in the temple.

寂しさや須磨<ruby>須磨<rt>すま</rt></ruby>にかちたる浜の秋

How lonely it is!
Even lonelier than Suma,
Autumn at this beach.

〈大垣〉

露通も此みなとまで出むかひて、みのゝ国へと伴ふ。駒にたすけられて大垣の庄に入ば、曾良も伊勢より来り合、越人も馬をとばせて、如行が家に入集る。前川子、荊口父子、其外したしき人々日夜とぶらひて、蘇生のものにあふがごとく、且悦び、且いたはる。旅の物うさもいまだやまざるに、長月六日になれば、伊勢の遷宮おがまんと、又舟にのりて、

　　蛤のふたみにわかれ行秋ぞ

174

Rotsū came all the way to Tsuruga to welcome me back, and we journeyed together to the province of Mino. The journey was made easier by having horses to ride. When we arrived at Ōgaki manor we were joined by Sora, who had come from Ise. Etsujin had also hurried here by horse, and we had a reunion at Jokō's house. All day and night dear friends—Zensenshi, Keikō and his son, and others—came to visit. They seemed as happy and solicitous as if they had encountered someone returned from the dead.

Before I had entirely recovered from the fatigue of the journey, I left on the sixth of the ninth month to witness the renewal of the Great Shrine at Ise. As I once again boarded a boat, I wrote:

> hamaguri no Dividing like clam
> Futami ni wakare And shell, I leave for Futami—
> yuku aki zo Autumn is passing by.[56]

蛤(はまぐり)のふたみにわかれ行秋(ゆく)ぞ

Dividing like clam
And shell, I leave for Futami—
Autumn is passing by.

脚 注

1. 芭蕉は明らかに、家を小さな娘を持つ男に売っている。桃の節句にはこの家には雛が飾られたであろう。しかし、独身の芭蕉が住んでいた間は、雛などは飾ったこともなかった。

2. 日付は、原文と同じく、すべて太陰暦で示してある。芭蕉が江戸を発ったのは、太陽歴では、5月16日であった。

3. 西洋歴では、1689年。

4. 木花之開耶姫は皇室の祖である瓊瓊杵尊の妻となるが、一夜を共に過ごしただけで身ごもる。そのため、瓊瓊杵の疑惑をかう。そこで、火中に身を投じ、この火中で子供が無事生まれるなら、自分がほかの男を知らないことの証明になろうと言う。そして無事三神を生む。芭蕉はここでは、その一人、火火出見尊に言及している。

5. このしろはニシン科の魚で、焼くと、人を火葬にしたときのようなにおいがしたという。

6. 芭蕉は、日光の東照宮にふれ、徳川家のもたらした平和と繁栄を誉め称える。つぎの句の「日の光」は、日光からもたらされる恵みを指している。

7. 日本では、太陰暦の夏の始まり、4月1日に衣更をするのが習慣だった。ここではもう一つの意味がある。曽良が、出家して頭を剃り、墨衣に着替えたことである。

8. 芭蕉はバナナの一種であるが、実をもたない。その葉は風が吹いてもたやすく裂けることで珍重され、それゆえ詩人を象徴する。芭蕉庵の庭には芭蕉があり、俳人はそれを自分の号とした。

9. 僧侶たちは旧暦4月16日から90日間、独居房に閉じこもって写経などの修行に励む。芭蕉も、旅の出発にあたって、俗世間から隠遁するような気持ちになったかもしれない。

FOOTNOTES

1. Bashō apparently sold his house to a man with small daughters. At the time of the Feast of Peach Blossoms (momo no sekku), dolls would be displayed in the house; but as long as Bashō, a bachelor, lived there dolls had not been displayed.

2. All dates are given (as in the original) in accordance with the lunar calendar. By the solar calendar, Bashō left Edo on the sixteenth of May.

3. 1689 by the Western calendar.

4. The goddess, Konohana Sakuya Hime, became the consort of Ninigi no Mikoto, the direct ancestor of the imperial line. She conceived after they had spent only one night together. This aroused the suspicion of Ninigi. She subjected herself to this test of fire, saying that if the child was born healthy despite the fire, it would prove she had not known any other man. She safely gave birth to three gods, one of whom, Hohodemi ("Fire Bright"), is mentioned by Bashō.

5. The fish, a kind of shad, when broiled is said to give off a smell like burning human flesh (at a cremation).

6. Bashō is referring to the mausoleum of the Tokugawa shoguns at Nikkō, and expressing his deep appreciation of the peace and prosperity which this family has brought Japan. In the following poem the "light of the sun" (hi no hikari) refers to the blessings emanating from Nikkō.

7. It was customary in Japan to change to summer attire on the first day of the fourth month, the beginning of summer according to the lunar calendar. There is a second meaning: Sora has shaved his head in order to look like a Buddhist priest, and has also changed from civilian to priestly clothes.

8. The bashō is a kind of banana tree, but it bears no fruit. It is prized because the leaves are easily torn by the wind, and therefore symbolizes the poet. There was a bashō tree in Bashō's garden, and he took his name from the tree.

9. For a period of ninety days (beginning on the sixteenth of the fourth month), priests shut themselves up within their cells and spent the time copying sutras and other religious practices. Bashō may have felt at the start of his journey that he too was beginning a "retreat" from worldly affairs.

10. 当時の日本の若い女性は、地味だが、「八重」がとりわけ愛らしい、撫子に
    たとえられた。今でも使われることがある。

11. 芭蕉はここで、『平家物語』の十一章の有名な下りを思い出している。弓の
    名人、那須与一は、250フィートも先の浪のゆれる船上の扇を射ることを
    命じられる。八幡に祈った与一は、もし射損じたら自決するつもりであっ
    たが、その矢は扇を見事に射抜いたのであった。

12. 芭蕉は、陸奥への旅にあたって、脚が強くなるよう、諸国を縦横に旅した
    七世紀の僧、役行者の像に祈った。役行者は、多くの人々に、自分の打ち
    立てた修験道の苦行に励むよう説得したという。

13. 仏頂（1643?–1715）。芭蕉が師事した禅僧。

14. 芭蕉は、二人の中国の僧の洞窟にふれている。原妙はその洞窟に15年止ま
    り、死ぬまでそこを出なかった。法雲は、巨岩に作った差し掛け小屋に住
    んだという。

15. これらの語は、芭蕉の讃えてやまない大歌人西行の歌に出てくる。芭蕉が
    奥の細道の旅の出発に1689年を選んだのは、この年が西行没後500年であ
    ったためらしい。

16. 平兼盛（990年没）作「便あらばいかで都へ告やらんけふ白川のせきはこゆる
    と」。『拾遺集』に納められている。

17. この逸話は、藤原清輔（1104–1177）の著した『袋草紙』にでてくる。

18. 阿弥陀仏の極楽浄土。

19. 芭蕉が花かつみに興味を持ったのは『古今集』（677）の詠み人知らず「みちの
    くのあさかの沼の花かつみかつ見る人に恋ひやわたらん」からであった。
    花かつみは、よくアヤメの一種と間違えられる。

20. 多くが、鯉の形をした紙のぼり。今日でも、男の子の生まれた家では、5
    月5日に家の外に飾る。

21. 藤原実方（998年没）は平安中期の歌人。985年、左近衛中将に任命されるが、
    藤原行成（972–1027）との口論をとがめられ、陸奥の守に左遷され、その地
    で没した。

10. Young Japanese women were (and occasionally still are) referred to as yaenadeshiko, an unassuming but lovely flower, particularly attractive when "double."

11. Bashō is here recalling a celebrated passage from Chapter 11 of *The Tale of the Heike*. Nasu no Yoichi, celebrated for his skill as a bowman, is commanded to shoot a fan on a moving boat some two hundred and fifty feet away. He prays to Hachiman, declaring that if his arrow misses the target he will commit suicide; but his arrow hits the fan squarely.

12. Bashō was praying before the statue of En no Gyōja, a seventh-century priest who traveled to virtually every corner of the country, for strong legs, needed on his journey to the far north. En no Gyōja persuaded many others to follow the ascetic practices of shugendō, as his cult was known.

13. A Zen priest (1643?–1715) with whom Bashō studied.

14. Bashō is referring to the hermitages of two Chinese priests. Genmyō (Yuan-miao in Chinese) remained for fifteen years in his hut, determined not to leave it until his death. Hōun (or Fa-yun) lived in a lean-to he built next to a boulder.

15. The words occur in a waka by the celebrated priest-poet Saigyō, a man for whom Bashō had the greatest admiration. It seems likely that Bashō embarked on his journey to the north in 1689 because it was five hundred years since the death of Saigyō.

16. The poet was Taira no Kanemori (d.990). The poem in question appears in the imperially sponsored anthology *Shūi Shū*.

17. The anecdote appears in Fukurozōshi, a collection of anecdotes compiled by Fujiwara no Kiyosuke (1104–1177).

18. The paradise of Amida Buddha.

19. Bashō's interest in the water-oat (hanagatsumi) was probably inspired by the anonymous poem in the Kokinshū (677): "Michinoku no Asaka no numa no hanaga-tsumi katsu miru hito ni koi ya wataran" (My love goes on for the person I have so seldom met, rare as the sight of flowering water-oats in the marsh of Asaka in Michinoku.) The hanagatsumi has often been mistakenly identified as a species of iris.

20. Banners, often in the shape of a carp, are still displayed on May 5 outside houses where a boy has been born.

21. Fujiwara no Sanekata (d. 998) was a Heian-period poet. He became a "middle captain" (chūjō) in 985. A quarrel with Fujiwara no Yukinari (972–1027) led to his being exiled to Oku, where he died.

22. 「かた見の薄」は『新古今集』798番の西行の歌からひいたもの。その歌の詞書きで、西行は、「陸奥の旅で荒れ果てた塚に至り、それが実方の塚であることを知った」と書いている。

23. 『後拾遺集』1043番の能因法師の歌は、二度目に訪れたとき、武隈の松は跡形もなくなっていたと詠んでいる。その松は、1000年という生涯を終えたのであろうが、私もそんな年になったのかと感慨に耽る。

24. 『古今集』1091番、詠み人知らず。

25. 壺とはポットかボウルのようなものであるが、壺の碑は壺には似ても似つかない形をしている。この場合の「つぼ」は地名で、この碑のある村の名前であろう。

26. この山は末の松山といい、寺は末松寺である。音は似ていないが、同じ漢字を、前者は訓読みに、後者は音読みにしている。

27. 『古今集』1088番、詠み人知らず。

28. 芭蕉は、琵琶の伴奏で語る『平家物語』と、英雄譚にあわせて舞う幸若舞に言及している。

29. 芭蕉は、中国の儒家韓癒 (768–824) を引用する。出典は、中国の有名な文集『古文真宝後集』であろう。

30. 『万葉集』4097番、大伴家持の歌の引用。陸奥に砂金が発見されたことを祝う歌の反歌として、749年に詠まれた。

31. 袖のわたり、尾ぶちの牧、まのの萱はらは歌枕で、古い歌によく使われた。

32. 杜甫 (712–770) の詩の引用で、日本語訳はことわざのように有名になった。

33. 兼房は義経の年老いた家臣。義経自害ののち、その妻と子供たちを殺し、館に火を放って、敵の残党狩りをくらました。

34. ふたたび杜甫の詩の引用。

35. 明らかに、『古今集』1092番、「もがみ川のぼればくだるいな舟のいなにはあらず此月ばかり」をさしている。この詠み人知らずには、「いな舟」という語が入っている。

22. The poem in question, by Saigyō, is #798 in the *Shin Kokinshū*. In the preface to the poem Saigyō describes how, while on a journey to Michinoku, he had come across an untended burial mound and learned that Sanekata was buried there.

23. Nōin's poem, #1043 in the anthology *Go Shūi Shū*, states that on visiting the Takekuma Pine for a second time, it had disappeared completely. He supposes that the pine had died on attaining its full longevity of a thousand years, and wonders if he too had reached that age.

24. From an anonymous poem, #1091 in the *Kokinshū*.

25. The word tsubo means a pot or a bowl, but the monument (which survives) in no way resembles a pot; probably tsubo is a place-name, the name of the village where the monument originally stood.

26. The mountain is called Sue no Matsu Yama, and the temple Masshōji. These do not look alike, but the former is the Japanese, and the latter the Sino-Japanese pronunciation of the same characters.

27. This is the anonymous poem #1088 in the *Kokinshū*.

28. Bashō refers to the recitation of sections of *Heike Monogatari* to the accompaniment of a biwa, and to kōwaka-mai, dances that went with the recitation of texts describing heroic deeds.

29. Bashō is quoting the Chinese Confucian thinker Han Yu (768–824). Probably his source was the anthology *Kobun Shimpō Kōshū*, a popular compendium of Chinese literary and philosophical materials.

30. The quotation is from poem #4097 in the *Man'yōshū* by Ōtomo no Yakamochi. It was composed in 749 as the "envoy" to a poem celebrating the discovery of gold in Michinoku.

31. Sode no Watashi, Obuchi no Maki, and Mano no Kayahara were utamakura, places often mentioned in the old poetry.

32. A quotation from a poem by Tu Fu (712–770) which became in Japanese translation a proverbial expression.

33. Kanefusa was an aged retainer of Yoshitsune. It was he who, after Yoshitsune's suicide, killed Yoshitsune's wife and children, then set fire to the building containing the corpses, in this way cheating the enemy of their remains.

34. Another quotation from Tu Fu.

35. Apparently a reference to poem #1092 in the *Kokinshū*. This anonymous poem contains the word inabune, or "rice boat."

36. 927年に撰進された律令の施行細則。

37. これと前の文に、芭蕉が羽黒の語源をどう考えたかが示されている。黒いという字は、里と山と解釈しうる点4つでできている。羽州はここにみるように、出羽と呼ばれていた。

38. 木綿しめと宝冠は、入山者の正装の一部。

39. 古代中国の最も有名な2本の剣。もとは、作者の刀工とその妻の名であった。

40. 行尊（1057–1135）は天台の高僧で、歌人でもあった。ここで芭蕉が言及している歌は、『金葉集』（1125年ごろ）にとられている。「もろともにあはれと思へ山ざくら花より外にしる人もなし」

41. 寺の名前干満珠寺は、神功后宮が三韓征伐のとき、潮の干満を司る真珠を持っていたという伝説に由来する。

42. 西施は、中国の有名な美女で、とりわけその悩める表情で知られる。「ねぶ」は、「眠る」と「眠り草」をかけている。

43. 「祭礼」は次行の俳句のタイトル。

44. 曽良は、その地の古い習慣に感動し、祭りにはどんな古い料理を食べるのだろうと思う。

45. 岐阜の商人で、俳句を作るときは低耳という号を用いた。『奥の細道』では、芭蕉と曽良以外の句は、これ一句だけである。

46. 旧暦7月7日は七夕で、二つの星が年に一度相まみえる祭りである。そのことを思うと、前日の6日も、ただの日とは思えない。

47. これらの難所では、波が突然道路を洗って胆を冷やすので、人はいちばん身近な者さえ忘れるし、動物は思わず引き返すという。

48. 芭蕉は、このようにして、自分にとって特別に大切な二つの寺、那智の青岸渡寺（那智観音堂）と谷汲の華厳寺の名前を結びつけた。

49. この句は、那谷の石は琵琶湖近くの石山寺の石より白いと言おうとしている、と解釈される。しかし、石山寺の石は黒いので、たいていの寺の石はそれよりも白いだろう。そこの説明が必要である。道教では、秋は白で表す。

36. A collection of ceremonies, prayers, usages, etc., compiled in 927.

37. This and the preceding sentence represent Bashō's speculations about the origin of the name Haguro. The character kuro contains sato and four dots that might be construed as yama. Ushū (province of feathers) is normally called Dewa, as in the following.

38. The paper cords (yūshime) and the sacred crowns (hōkan) formed part of the attire of pilgrims.

39. The names of the two most famous swords of ancient China; originally, these were the names of the swordsmith and his wife who made the swords.

40. Gyōson (1057–1135) was a high-ranking Tendai Priest who was also known as a poet. The poem to which Bashō refers is in the collection Kin'yōshū (c. 1125). The general sense of the poem is: "Mountain cherry, share my feelings; except for your blossoms there is no one here."

41. The name of the temple (Kanmanju-ji) is a reference to the legend that the Empress Jingū had pearls that controlled the tide which she used to good advantage during her expedition against Korea.

42. A celebrated Chinese beauty (Hsi Shih), known especially for her mournful expression. There is a pun on nebu (to sleep) and nebu (mimosa).

43. The word sairei is apparently a title for the haiku that follows.

44. Sora, apparently impressed by the antiquity of the place, wonders what ancient food is eaten at the festival.

45. A merchant from Gifu who used Teiji as his name when he wrote poetry. This is the only poem in the work not by either Bashō or Sora.

46. The seventh night of the seventh month was Tanabata, the festival of the two stars that meet once a year. Even the sixth has something special about its atmosphere.

47. These were all places on the coast where onrushing waves suddenly would engulf the road, a place so frightening that people forgot even those dearest to them and animals turned back.

48. He was combining in this way the names of two temples with special importance for himself, Seigando-ji at Nachi and Kegon-ji at Tanigumi.

49. The poem is generally explained as meaning that the stones at Nata are whiter than those in the Ishiyama-dera near Lake Biwa. However, the stones there are black; the stones of almost any temple would be whiter than those of the Ishiyama-dera. Further elucidation is needed. White was the color of autumn in the Taoist system of correspondences.

50. 中国とその影響を受けている日本では、菊の香は治療効果があるとされている。

51. 安原貞室(1610–1673)は、松永貞徳(1571–1653)の弟子で、初期俳諧の代表作家である。

52. 旅の仲間が、笠の内側に「同行二人」などと書くならわしがあったが、曽良と別れてしまった今、芭蕉はこの文字を消してしまうであろう。

53. 夏も終わりなので、扇にものを書いて破り捨てようとするが、捨てがたい。扇を捨てがたいのは、北枝との別れと同じことだ。

54. あきらかに、『源氏物語』の「夕顔」の巻で、光源氏が夕顔を訪問する場面をひいている。

55. 遊行の行いは、その願いを叶えてくれるであろう神々を喜ばせるためであった。

56. この句は、最初の「行く春や・・・」に響きあう。「蛤のふた」は、伊勢大神宮近くの「二見」と掛詞になっている。

50. It was believed in China (and in Japan, under Chinese influence) that the scent of chrysanthemums had therapeutic value.

51. Yasuhara Teishitsu (1610–1673) studied haikai poetry with Matsunaga Teitoku (1571–1653) and became one of the important early poets of haikai.

52. It was customary for traveling companions to write inscriptions such as "two travelers in heaven and earth" inside their hats; but now that Sora is no longer with him, Bashō will wipe out these words.

53. Bashō, about to throw away his fan, now that summer had ended, impulsively scribbled something on it; but now it is hard to throw away. This reluctance to part with the fan echoes his reluctance to leave Hokushi.

54. Apparently a reference to the scene in the "Yūgao" chapter of *The Tale of Genji* in which Genji calls on Yūgao.

55. The actions of the Pilgrim-Priest (yugyō) were intended to please the gods, who would then be disposed to granting his request for a favor.

56. This verse echoes the first of the journey (yuku haru ya). It contains a kakekotoba on hamaguri no futa, meaning the shell of the clam, and Futami, the region around the Great Shrine at Ise.

対訳　おくのほそ道
The Narrow Road to Oku

1996年10月25日　第 1 刷発行
2005年 1 月27日　第10刷発行

切り絵	宮田雅之
英　訳	ドナルド・キーン
企画協力	宮田雅之アートプロモーション 株式会社雅房・瀧愁麗
発行者	畑野文夫
発行所	講談社インターナショナル株式会社 〒112-8652 東京都文京区音羽 1-17-14 電話　03-3944-6493（編集部） 　　　03-3944-6492（営業部・業務部） ホームページ　www.kodansha-intl.com
印刷所	光村印刷株式会社
製本所	株式会社 国宝社